Singapore Math® Intensive Practice is a series of 12 books written to provide challenging supplementary material for Singapore math programs.

The primary objective of this series of books is to help students generate greater interest in mathematics and gain more confidence in solving mathematical problems. To achieve this, special features are incorporated in the series.

SPECIAL FEATURES

Topical Review
Enables students of mixed abilities to be exposed to a good variety of questions which are of varying levels of difficulty so as to help them develop a better understanding of mathematical concepts and their applications.

Mid-Year or End-Of-Year Review
Provides students with a good review that summar_____ in Singapore math programs.

Take the Challenge!
Deepens students' mathematical concepts an_____ their mathematical reasoning and higher-order thinking skills as they practic_____ problem-solving strategies.

More Challenging Problems
Stimulate students' interest through challenging and thought-provoking problems which encourage them to think critically and creatively as they apply their knowledge and experience in solving these problems.

Why this Series?
Students will find this series of books a good complement and supplement to Singapore math programs. The comprehensive coverage certainly makes this series a valuable resource for teachers, parents and tutors.

It is hoped that the special features in this series of books will inspire and spur young people to achieve better mathematical competency and greater mathematics problem-solving skills.

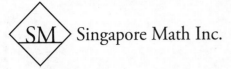
Singapore Math Inc.

Copyright © 2004 Singapore Math Inc.

Published by
Singapore Math Inc.
19535 SW 129th Ave.
Tualatin, OR 97062
U.S.A.
E-mail: customerservice@singaporemath.com
www.singaporemath.com

First published 2004
Reprinted 2005, 2006, 2007, 2008, 2009, 2010, 2012, 2013,
2014, 2016, 2018, 2019, 2020

Singapore Math® Intensive Practice 5B
ISBN 978-1-932906-09-7

Printed in China

Our special thanks to Jenny Kempe for her assistance in editing
Singapore Math® Intensive Practice.

Intensive Practice 5B

Contents

Topic 1: Decimals

1. Fill in each blank with a decimal.

   (a) 1 ten, 5 tenths, 7 hundredths and 8 thousandths   10.578

   (b) 2 ones, 48 tenths and 5 hundredths   6.85

   (c) 8 ones, 3 tenths, 61 hundredths and 2 thousandths   8.912

   (d) $14.375 = 14 +$ ____0.375____

   (e) ____20.796____ $= 20 + 0.7 + 0.09 + 0.006$

   (f) $1.2 +$ ____0.06____ $+ 0.008 = 1.268$

2. Fill in the blanks.

   (a) The numeral 7.361 is made up of 7 ones, 3 tenths and ____61____ thousandths.

   (b) In the numeral 11.048, there are ____2____ hundredths, 11 ones, 28 thousandths and 0 tenths.

   (c) In the number 31.869, what is the

      (i) digit in the hundredths place,   6

      (ii) value of the digit '3',   30

      (iii) value of the digit '9',   0.009

      (iv) digit in the tenths place?   8

3. Write the value of each of the following as a decimal.

   (a) $\dfrac{3}{10} + \dfrac{2}{100} + \dfrac{1}{1000} =$ ____0.321____

   (b) $\dfrac{1}{2} + 0.07 + \dfrac{8}{1000} =$ ____0.578____

   (c) $5.7 + \dfrac{33}{100} + \dfrac{61}{1000} =$ ____6.091____

4. Arrange the following numbers in increasing order.

(a) $3\frac{1}{3}$, 3.03, $3\frac{3}{5}$, 3.3̇1̇3 → over them: 3, 1, 4, 2   _3.03, 3.313, 3 1/3, 3 3/5_

(b) 68.9, $6\frac{89}{100}$, 689.9, $6\frac{9}{10}$ → over: 3, 1, 4, 2   _6 89/100, 6 9/10, 68.9, 689.9_

(c) 3.375, $2\frac{2}{3}$, 3.75, $3\frac{4}{9}$ → over: 2, 1, 4, 3   _2 2/3, 3.75, 3 4/9, 3.75_

5. Round off each number to the nearest whole number.

(a) 5.901 ___6___ (b) 3.499 ___3___

(c) 21.47 ___21___ (d) 125.86 ___126___

6. Round off each number to 1 decimal place.

(a) 0.56 ___0.6___ (b) 1.905 ___1.9___

(c) 32.97 ___33.0___ (d) 65.086 ___65.1___

7. Round off each number to 2 decimal places.

(a) 0.915 ___0.92___ (b) 3.207 ___3.21___

(c) 40.995 ___41.00___ (d) 99.969 ___99.97___

8. Divide and give each answer as a decimal correct to 2 decimal places.

(a) $13 \div 3 \approx$ _4.33_ (b) $33 \div 7 \approx$ _4.71_

(c) $29 \div 6 \approx$ _4.83_ (d) $19 \div 8 \approx$ _2.38_

9. Express each fraction as a decimal correct to 2 decimal places.

(a) $\frac{4}{9} \approx$ _0.44_ (b) $1\frac{2}{7} \approx$ _1.29_

(c) $\frac{8}{3} \approx$ _2.67_ (d) $7\frac{7}{8} \approx$ _7.88_

10. Express each decimal as a fraction in its simplest form.

(a) 0.175 _7/40_ (b) 2.68 _2 17/25_

(c) 3.55 _3 11/20_ (d) 9.375 _9 3/8_

11. Divide and give each answer correct to 2 decimal places.

(a) $48.03 \div 7 \approx$

$$
\begin{array}{r}
0\,6.8\,6 \\
7\,\overline{)\,48.03} \\
0 \\
\overline{4\,8} \\
4\,2 \\
\overline{6.0} \\
5\,6 \\
\overline{4\,3} \\
4\,2 \\
\overline{1}
\end{array}
$$

(b) $83.26 \div 9 \approx$

$$
\begin{array}{r}
0\,9.2\,5 \\
9\,\overline{)\,83.26} \\
0 \\
\overline{8\,3} \\
8\,1 \\
\overline{2\,2} \\
1\,8 \\
\overline{4\,6} \\
4\,5 \\
\overline{1}
\end{array}
$$

(c) $0.71 \div 6 \approx 0.12$

$$
\begin{array}{r}
0.1\,1\,\,{}^{A5}\approx 0.12 \\
6\,\overline{)\,0.71} \\
0 \\
\overline{0.7} \\
6 \\
\overline{1\,1} \\
6 \\
\overline{5}
\end{array}
$$

(d) $100.36 \div 5 \approx$

$$
\begin{array}{r}
0\,2\,0.0\,7 \\
5\,\overline{)\,100.36} \\
6 \\
\overline{1\,0} \\
1\,0 \\
\overline{0\,0} \\
0 \\
\overline{0\,0.3} \\
0 \\
\overline{3\,6} \\
3\,5 \\
\overline{1}
\end{array}
$$

12. Work out these problems.

(a) Seven children share $5.00 equally. How much does each child get, to the nearest ten cents?

$$
\begin{array}{r}
0.7\,1 \\
7\,\overline{)\,5.00} \\
0 \\
\overline{5\,0} \\
4\,4 \\
\overline{1\,0} \\
7 \\
\overline{3}
\end{array}
$$

70¢

(b) A grocer bought a sack of rice which weighed 49.87 kg. He packed it into 6 bags. Each bag of rice weighed as heavy as each of the other bags. How much did each bag of rice weigh? Give the answer in kilograms correct to 2 decimal places.

$$
\begin{array}{r}
0\,8.1\,4 \quad\approx 8.10 \\
6\,\overline{)\,49.87} \\
0 \\
\overline{4\,8} \\
4\,8 \\
\overline{.8}
\end{array}
$$

(c) Arlene mixed 13.63 ℓ of lemonade with 39.95 ℓ of limeade to make limeade juice. She then poured the mixture into 8 containers. How much juice did each container hold? Give the answer in liters, correct to 2 decimal places.

$$
\begin{array}{r}
13.63 \\
+\,39.95 \\
\hline
53.58
\end{array}
$$

$$
\begin{array}{r}
0\,6.6\,9 \rightarrow 6.70\ \ell \\
8\,\overline{)\,53.58} \\
0 \\
\overline{5\,3} \\
4\,8 \\
\overline{5.5} \\
4.8 \\
\overline{7\,8} \\
7\,2 \\
\overline{6}
\end{array}
$$

3

13. Fill in the blanks.

   (a) 4.73 × _____ = 47.3

   (b) 40.94 × _____ = 409.4

   (c) 3.14 × 20 = _____

   (d) 0.005 × 40 = _____

   (e) 0.43 × 80 = _____

   (f) 8.02 × 90 = _____

   (g) 37.18 × 60 = _____

   (h) 3.079 × 70 = _____

14. Fill in the blanks.

   (a) 1.709 × _____ = 170.9

   (b) 16.325 × _____ = 1632.5

   (c) 4.02 × 100 = _____

   (d) 0.055 × 300 – _____

   (e) 0.385 × 500 = _____

   (f) 6.03 × 400 = _____

   (g) 1.023 × 600 = _____

   (h) 3.142 × 800 = _____

15. Fill in the blanks.

   (a) 0.1472 × _____ = 147.2

   (b) 9.862 × _____ = 9862

   (c) 1.006 × 1000 = _____

   (d) 0.576 × 2000 = _____

   (e) 7.28 × 6000 = _____

   (f) 0.099 × 4000 = _____

   (g) 5.034 × 7000 = _____

   (h) 67.42 × 9000 = _____

16. Find the missing numbers.

   (a) 8 ÷ _____ = 0.8

   (b) 59.33 ÷ _____ = 5.933

   (c) 0.48 ÷ 40 = _____

   (d) 35.6 ÷ 50 = _____

   (e) 4.2 ÷ 60 = _____

   (f) 78.4 ÷ 70 = _____

   (g) 324 ÷ 80 = _____

   (h) 413.1 ÷ 90 = _____

17. Find the missing numbers.

   (a) 3.8 ÷ _____ = 0.038

   (b) 48.2 ÷ _____ = 0.482

   (c) 7 ÷ 200 = _____

   (d) 192.4 ÷ 100 = _____

   (e) 48.6 ÷ 600 = _____

   (f) 215.6 ÷ 700 = _____

   (g) 784 ÷ 400 = _____

   (h) 327.2 ÷ 800 = _____

18. Find the missing numbers.

(a) $85 \div \underline{1000} = 0.085$ (b) $7021 \div \underline{1000} = 7.021$

(c) $7 \div 1000 = \underline{0.007}$ (d) $234 \div 2000 = \underline{0.117}$

(e) $9060 \div 6000 = \underline{1.51}$ (f) $1475 \div 5000 = \underline{0.295}$

(g) $434 \div 7000 = \underline{0.062}$ (h) $13{,}662 \div 9000 = \underline{1.518}$

19. Work out these problems.

(a) Each book weighs 0.35 kg. How much do 1000 of these books weigh?

$$0.35$$
$$\times \ 10$$
$$\overline{035} = 35 \times 10 = 350$$

(b) Mark runs 10 times round the border of his school field. If he runs a total distance of 4.8 mi, find the perimeter of the school field in miles.

(c) How many liters of coke are there in 100 cans if each can contains 0.385 liters of coke? Give your answer to the nearest liter.

39 liters

(d) A man donated a total of $137,888 to 1000 needy children. If each of these children received an equal amount of money, how much did each child receive? Give the answer correct to the nearest cent.

(e) At a supermarket, meat is sold at $1.38 for 100 g of it. How much do I have to pay for 2 kg of the meat?

5

20. Estimate the value of each of the following.

    (a) $0.4 \times 35 \approx$ _____

    (b) $7.4 \times 82 \approx$ _____

    (c) $18.7 \times 66 \approx$ _____

    (d) $87.03 \times 29 \approx$ _____

    (e) $3.79 \times 40.12 \approx$ _____

    (f) $604.7 \times 57 \approx$ _____

    (g) $39.97 \times 12.89 \approx$ _____

    (h) $49.81 \times 98.95 \approx$ _____

21. Multiply.

    (a) $2.8 \times 34 =$ _____

    (b) $0.37 \times 48 =$ _____

$$\begin{array}{r} 2\,.\,8 \\ \times\quad 3\ 4 \\ \hline \end{array}$$

$$\begin{array}{r} 0\,.\,3\,7 \\ \times\quad\ 4\,8 \\ \hline \end{array}$$

    (c) $9.37 \times 56 =$ _____

    (d) $93.27 \times 85 =$ _____

$$\begin{array}{r} 9\,.\,3\,7 \\ \times\quad\ 5\,6 \\ \hline \end{array}$$

$$\begin{array}{r} 9\,3\,.\,2\,7 \\ \times\quad\ 8\,5 \\ \hline \end{array}$$

    (e) $23 \times 29.99 =$ _____

    (f) $12 \times 15.45 =$ _____

$$\begin{array}{r} 2\,9\,.\,9\,9 \\ \times\quad\ 2\,3 \\ \hline \end{array}$$

$$\begin{array}{r} 1\,5\,.\,4\,5 \\ \times\quad\ 1\,2 \\ \hline \end{array}$$

22. Work out these problems.

    (a)   Mrs. Connelly bought 12 pens for $21.00. She also bought 8 pairs of scissors. She gave the cashier $50 and received a change of $7.40. What was the cost of each pair of scissors?

(b)　A bottle contains 0.414 ℓ of liquid soap. Two dozens of such bottles of liquid soap are poured into 2-liter dispensers. At least how many dispensers are required to hold all the liquid soap?

(c)　Denise used 1.6 yd of ribbon to tie a present. She tied a total of 55 presents in the same manner. How much did she pay for the ribbon if 1 yd of the ribbon cost $0.45?

(d)　1 lb of prawns costs $17.90 and 1 lb of crab meat costs $10.95. Mrs. Ong wants to buy 15 lb of prawns and 12 lb of crab meat. How much does she have to pay for them?

(e)　A class of 37 students collected a total of $5875 for their school building fund. If each student collected about the same amount of money, estimate the amount each student collected.

23.　Find the equivalent measures.

(a)　2.45 km = _____ m

(b)　0.038 km = _____ m

(c)　0.75 ft = _____ in.

(d)　1.56 m = _____ cm

(e)　0.671 kg = _____ g

(f)　10.53 kg = _____ g

(g)　$1.29 = _____ ¢

(h)　$46.25 = _____ ¢

(i)　6.103 ℓ = _____ ml

(j)　0.75 gal = _____ c

24. Find the equivalent measures in compound units.

   (a)   9.81 m = _____ m _____ cm

   (b)   21.35 m = _____ m _____ cm

   (c)   8.027 ℓ = _____ ℓ _____ ml

   (d)   10.5 ft = _____ ft _____ in.

   (e)   1.439 km = _____ km _____ m

   (f)   45.125 lb = _____ lb _____ oz

   (g)   0.55 kg = _____ kg _____ g

   (h)   13.904 kg = _____ kg _____ g

25. Find the equivalent measures. Express each answer as a decimal.

   (a)   709 m = _____ km   (b)   4054 m = _____ km

   (c)   8 g = _____ kg   (d)   10,016 g = _____ kg

   (e)   3123 ml = _____ ℓ   (f)   8062 qt = _____ gal

   (g)   105 ¢ = $_____   (h)   11,769 ¢ = $_____

   (i)   24 cm = _____ m   (j)   1395 in. = _____ ft

26. Find the equivalent measures. Express each answer as a decimal.

   (a)   5 km 608 m = _____ km   (b)   10 km 47 m = _____ km

   (c)   3 kg 94 g = _____ kg   (d)   8 kg 106 g = _____ kg

   (e)   7 ℓ 5 ml = _____ ℓ   (f)   20 ℓ 175 ml = _____ ℓ

   (g)   10 lb 8 oz = _____ lb   (h)   603 in. = _____ ft

27. Work out these problems.

   (a)   3.6 kg of beef is cut into pieces with each piece weighing 200 g. How
         many pieces of beef are there?

8

(b)   0.6 liters of coffee was shared equally among 8 people. How many milliliters of coffee did each person get?

(c)   Mrs. Tansy buys some beef that weighs 4 kg 125 g. Mrs. Kerry buys some chicken that weighs 4.19 kg. Which of the meat is heavier?

(d)   A shopkeeper has a roll of raffia string that is 50 meters long. He cuts it into shorter lengths of 59 cm. How many of such shorter pieces of raffia strings can he get?

WORD PROBLEMS

1.   Sam bought two watermelons. One watermelon weighed 3.55 kg. It was 789 g lighter than the other watermelon. How much did the two watermelons weigh in all? Give the answer in kilograms.

2. Molly paid $93.60 for half a dozen reams of paper and a dozen pens. Each pen cost $3.85. Find the cost of each ream of paper.

3. Sean ordered 18 cartons of canned drinks. There were 24 cans in each carton. He paid $10.50 for each carton of the drinks. He then sold each can for $0.65. How much money did he make if all the cans were sold?

4. Mrs. Lim mixes 1.17 ℓ of milk with 4 times as much tea to make milk tea for her family. She pours the milk tea equally into 9 plastic cups. How much milk tea is there in each cup? Give the answer in liters.

5. A basket containing 3 bricks weighs 5.35 kg. If the same basket is filled with 7 bricks, it will weigh 9.55 kg. How much does the basket weigh when it is empty? Give the answer in kilograms.

6. A dressmaker used 2.36 yd of a roll of cloth to sew a skirt and $1\frac{1}{2}$ times as long to sew a dress. She sewed 8 skirts and 8 dresses. If she used a roll of cloth that was 50 yd long, what was the length of cloth that was left unused? Give the answer in yards.

7. (a) If 0.75 of a number is 120, what is the number?

   (b) What is the missing number in the box, correct to 2 decimal places?

   $\frac{1}{3}$ of $\boxed{}$ = 2.786

8. (a) Rose saved 0.8 of what Tom saved. If Tom saved $66 more than Rose, what was their total savings?

   (b) At an office party, 0.45 of the people were women. If there were 24 more men than women, how many people attended the party?

9. The area of a triangle is 0.2 of the area of a square. A rectangle has an area 0.7 times the area of the square. The total area of the triangle, square and rectangle is 494 cm^2. What is the difference in area between the triangle and the rectangle?

10. A plumber cut a pipe into 5 equal pieces and had 27 cm of the pipe left. For a second pipe 15 m long, he cut 11 pieces of the same length as that of each piece cut from the first pipe and had 15 cm of the second pipe left.
    (a) What was the length of each shorter piece of the second pipe?
    (b) What was the total length of the two pipes, in meters?

11. The total cost of 5 CDs and 3 video tapes was $169.20. The total cost of a CD and a video tape was $43.80. If I bought 3 CDs and 5 video tapes and paid with two $100 bills, how much change would I receive?

12. Karen had 0.8 times the amount of money Laura had. They went shopping and spent $684 altogether. Karen spent 0.25 of her money and had three times as much money left as Laura. How much money did Laura spend?

13. A transport company charges $0.60 for every pot safely delivered but pays a penalty charge of $27.35 for every pot that is broken or lost during the journey. If it delivered 500 pots for a customer, but lost 3 pots and broke 5 pots, how much money did the company collect altogether for the delivery?

14. 5 books and 9 magazines cost $150.50 altogether. 9 books and 5 magazines together cost $175.70. How much more does each book cost than each magazine?

15. The ratio of the area of a triangle to the area of a rectangle is 3 : 7. The triangle has a base of 15.3 cm and a height of 8 cm. If the width of the rectangle is 8.4 cm, find the perimeter of the rectangle.

Take the Challenge!

1. Insert 'x' or '÷' between the decimals to make the following number sentence true.

    0.1 ____ 0.5 ____ 0.6 ____ 0.12 ____ 0.2 ____ 0.25 ____ 0.5 ____ 0.1 = 1

2. An unstretched spring balance is 52 cm long. For every 0.02 kg of object supported by the spring balance, the spring stretches 0.15 cm. What will the length of the spring balance be when an object weighing 2.2 kg is hung on it?

2.2 kg

3. Convert the following recurring decimals into fractions.

   (a)   0.942424242…..

   (b)   1.3481481481481…..

   (c)   3.0405050505…..

Topic 2: Percentage

1. In a bag there are 50 shapes as shown below.

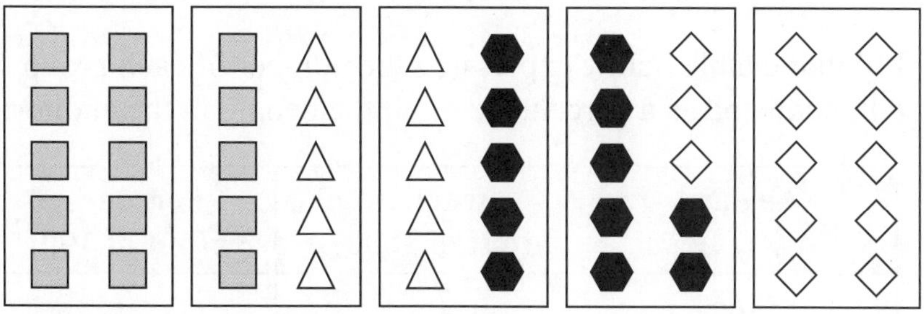

   (a) Fill in the table below expressing the number of each shape as a fraction and as a percentage of all the shapes in the bag.

Shape	Number of shapes	Fraction (out of 50)	Percentage (out of 100)
Square ▢			
Triangle △			
Hexagon ⬢			
Diamond ◇			

   Fill in the blanks.

   (b) 10 triangles and 12 hexagons make up _____% of the shapes in the bag.

   (c) All the squares and diamonds in the bag make up _____% of the shapes.

   (d) The percentage of triangles and squares in the bag is the same as the percentage of hexagons and diamonds and it is equal to _____%.

   (e) There are _____% more squares than triangles.

   (f) There are _____% more 4-sided shapes than non 4-sided shapes.

2. The following shows the number of people in an auditorium.

Men	450
Women	100
Boys	300
Girls	150
Total	1000

(a) Fill in the table below expressing the number of each group of people as a fraction and as a percentage of all the people in the auditorium.

Group	Fraction (out of 1000)	Percentage (out of 100)
Men		
Women		
Boys		
Girls		

(b) How many percent more adults than children are there? _____

(c) How many percent less female than male are there? _____

(d) All the women, 200 boys and 100 girls left the auditorium. What percentage of the people remained in the auditorium? _____

3. What percentage of each figure is shaded?

(a)   (b)   (c)

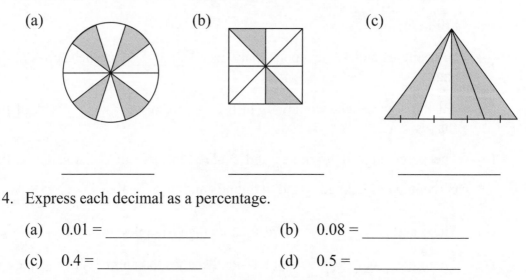

_____   _____   _____

4. Express each decimal as a percentage.

(a)   0.01 = _____   (b)   0.08 = _____

(c)   0.4 = _____   (d)   0.5 = _____

(e) 0.67 = _____   (f) 0.95 = _____

(g) 0.025 = _____   (h) 0.333 = _____

5. Express each fraction as a percentage.

(a) $\dfrac{23}{100}$ =   (b) $\dfrac{93}{100}$ =

(c) $\dfrac{2}{10}$ =   (d) $\dfrac{9}{10}$ =

(e) $\dfrac{21}{50}$ =   (f) $\dfrac{34}{50}$ =

(g) $\dfrac{12}{25}$ =   (h) $\dfrac{18}{25}$ =

(i) $\dfrac{13}{20}$ =   (j) $\dfrac{7}{20}$ =

(k) $\dfrac{1}{2}$ =   (l) $\dfrac{1}{8}$ =

(m) $\dfrac{3}{4}$ =   (n) $\dfrac{5}{8}$ −

6. Express each percentage as a decimal.

(a) 5% = _____   (b) 41% = _____

(c) 39% = _____   (d) 64% = _____

(e) 81% = _____   (f) 99% = _____

(g) 12.5% = _____   (h) 39.2% = _____

7. Express each percentage as a fraction in its simplest form.

(a) 6% = _____   (b) 12% = _____

(c) 25% = _____   (d) 56% = _____

(e) 15% = _____   (f) 40% = _____

(g) 37.5% = _____   (h) 94% = _____

8. Complete the percentage wall chart below.

Fraction	Decimal	Percentage
$\dfrac{1}{8}$		
$\dfrac{1}{4}$		
$\dfrac{1}{2}$		
$\dfrac{3}{4}$		
$\dfrac{1}{10}$		
$\dfrac{1}{20}$		
$\dfrac{1}{40}$		
$\dfrac{1}{100}$		

9. Work out these problems.

   (a)   89% of the students who took a math test passed. How many percent of the students did not pass?

   (b)   Davina took an English test. Out of 50 questions, she answered 44 correctly.
         (i)   What percentage of the questions did she answer correctly?
         (ii) What percentage of the questions did she answer wrongly?

   (c) $\dfrac{9}{20}$ of the fish in a pond are goldfish and the rest are koi. How many percent of the fish are koi?

(d) $\frac{1}{3}$ of the passengers on board an airplane are female. What percentage of the passengers are male? Express your answer as a mixed number.

(e) Out of 600 elementary school students, 48 are found to be obese.
  (i) What percentage of the students are obese?
  (ii) What percentage of the students are not obese?

(f) There were 96 flamingos in a pond at a bird park. 24 of them flew away.
  (i) What percentage of the birds flew away?
  (ii) What percentage of the birds remained in the pond?

(g) At the beach, $\frac{3}{5}$ of the people were children and $\frac{1}{2}$ of the rest of the people were women.
  (i) What percentage of the people present were children?
  (ii) What percentage of the people were men?

10. A farmer rears 540 fish in a pond. The table on the next page shows the different types of fish in the pond. How many of each type of fish does he have in the pond? Work out the answers and fill in the table.

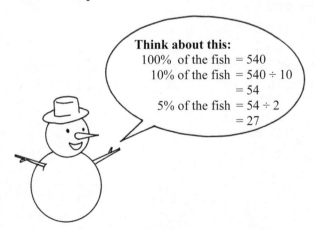

Think about this:
100% of the fish = 540
10% of the fish = 540 ÷ 10
= 54
5% of the fish = 54 ÷ 2
= 27

Type of fish	Percentage of the total number of fish in the pond	Number of fish
Tilapia	40%	
Grouper	25%	
Catfish	5%	
Pomfret	10%	
Carp	20%	

11. The table shows the different types of fruit juice that make up a can of soft drink. One such can holds 330 ml of soft drink. Work out the amount for each type of fruit juice in one can of soft drink.

Type of fruit juice	Percentage of the total amount of fruit juice in a can of drink	Amount of fruit juice (ml)
Orange	50%	
Lemon	35%	
Mango	10%	
Lime	5%	

12. Work out these problems.

(a) George had 50 liters of gas in his car's gas tank. He used 65% of the gas in 2 days. How much gas was used in the two days?

(b) Yvonne went shopping with $800. She spent 72% of her money on a handbag and a necklace. How much did she pay for the two items?

(c) Amy typed a letter that contained 150 words. 94% of the words in the letter were spelled correctly. How many words were spelled wrongly?

(d) A restaurant ordered 400 kg of beef for a dinner party. The cooks only used 89% of the beef. How much beef was not used?

(e) A rectangle is 20 cm long and 15 cm wide. 78% of the rectangle is colored green. Find the area of the rectangle that is not colored green.

(f) Last year, there were 120 road accidents. 85% of the accidents involved motorcyclists. How many accidents involved other road users?

13. Find the amount of interest in each of the following.

(a) Mrs. Hoon deposited $10,000 in a bank. The bank paid an interest of 4% per year.

Amount of interest earned in a year = 4% of $10,000

=

(b) Ken took up a car loan of $50,000 from ABC bank. The bank charged him 6% interest per year.

Amount of interest paid in a year = 6% of $50,000

=

(c) Mr. Lee took up a housing loan of $850,000 from XYZ bank. He had to pay an interest of 5% per year.

Amount of interest paid in a year = 5% of $850,000

=

14. Work out each of the following.

(a) Britney bought an evening dress from a boutique. The dress cost $1200. She was given a 15% discount.

Amount of discount given = 15% of $1200

=

(b) A set of white gold pendant and chain cost $182. Martha was given a discount of 20% for the set.

Amount of discount given = 20% of $182

=

(c) During a closing-down sale at a garment shop, the prices of all clothes were reduced by 70%. Zaleha bought some clothes that cost $575 before the discount.

Amount paid by Zaleha = 30% of $575

=

15. Work out the value of an 8% sales tax for each of the following items.

(a) A cell phone that costs $348 _____

(b) A tour package to Sydney that costs $3196 _____

16. Read the following example and work out the following problems.

    Example:

    Last year, there were 400 first grade students in a certain school. What will the enrollment be this year, if

    (i)   there is a 30% increase in the number of students this year?

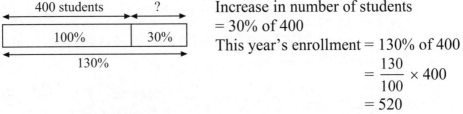

    Increase in number of students
    = 30% of 400
    This year's enrollment = 130% of 400
    $$= \frac{130}{100} \times 400$$
    $$= 520$$

    (ii) there is a 20% decrease in the number of students this year?

    Decrease in number of students
    = 20% of 400
    This year's enrollment = 80% of 400
    $$= \frac{80}{100} \times 400$$
    $$= 320$$

(a) The price of 5 lb of flour was 80 cents last year. There is a 5% increase in the price of flour this year. How much is this price increase?

    Price increase = 5% of 80 cents

    =

(b) Following part (a) above, the price of 5 lb of flour next year will be decreased by 5% from that of this year. How much will this price reduction be? Give the answer to the nearest cent.

    Price reduction =

(c) The population of a town called Burgundy was 45,000 last year. There is an increase of 20% in the population this year. What is the population this year?

Population this year =

(d) A number is decreased from 180 to 135. What is the percentage decrease?

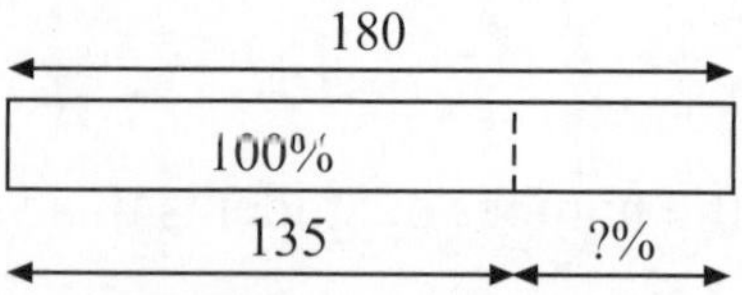

| 180 |
| 100% |
| 135 | ?% |

Decrease = 180 – 135 = 45

Percentage decrease =

(e) The volume of detergent in a box is increased from 7500 cm^3 to 8100 cm^3. What is the percentage increase in volume?

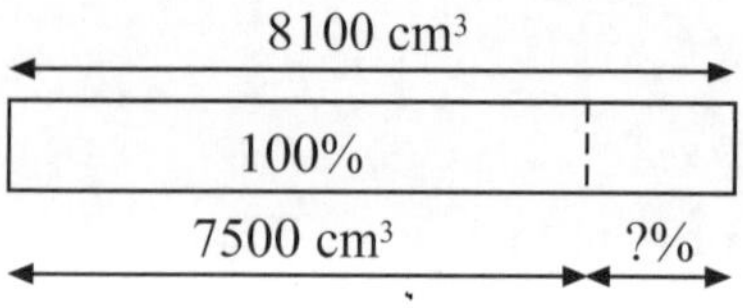

| 8100 cm³ |
| 100% |
| 7500 cm³ | ?% |

Increase in volume $= 8100 - 7500$
$= 600$ cm^3

Percentage increase =

17. Eight school soccer teams participated in a School Fantasy League. The results of their games are shown in the chart below.

Score \ Team	Challengers vs Boys United		Tiger Club vs Rovers		Kings vs Cougars		Dream Team vs Starlight	
	Challengers	Boys United	Tiger Club	Rovers	Kings	Cougars	Dream Team	Starlight
	1	1	0	1	1	0	1	1
Red Card	2	1	1	0	0	2	5	3
Corners	2	4	7	3	3	8	3	6
Fouls committed	10	15	16	10	9	10	14	28
Goal attempts	18	7	10	7	6	15	9	8

(a)   How many fouls in total were committed in the 4 games?

(b)   What percentage of all the fouls did the team with the most fouls commit?

(c)   How many red cards were shown to the players altogether?

(d)   Express the number of red cards flashed as a percentage of the total number of fouls committed.

(e)   How many attempts were made to score a goal throughout the 4 games?

(f)   Express the number of goals scored as a percentage of the total number of goal attempts.

WORD PROBLEMS

1. A notebook has 200 pages. Davina uses 28 pages of the notebook to write stories. What percentage of the notebook is not used?

2. Mrs. Magoo spent $\frac{3}{5}$ of her money in her purse on groceries and $\frac{1}{10}$ of it on some medicine. What percentage of her money in her purse did she have left?

3. In a math quiz, Jonathan answered more questions correctly than incorrectly. He answered 35% of the questions incorrectly. What was the percentage difference between the questions answered correctly and those answered incorrectly?

4. 75% of a class of 32 students were girls. 8 more boys joined the class in the second semester. What percentage of the class were boys?

5. ABCD is a rectangle of length 45 m and width 20 m. The area of triangle AEF is 33% of the area of ABCD. Find the area of triangle AEF.

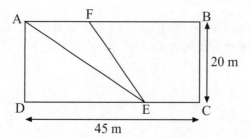

6. Mr. Macintosh bought 500 apples. He threw away 18% of the apples which were found rotten. If he sold the rest of the apples at 30 cents each, how much money did he collect from the sale?

7. Mr. Lim bought a van for $68,000. He borrowed this sum of money from a bank to pay for the van. The bank charged 4% interest per year.
If he paid off the loan in one year, how much did he have to pay?

8. There were 350 spaces in the parking lot of a shopping mall. The management of the shopping mall decided to reduce the number of spaces by 8%.
   (a) How many spaces were removed?
   (b) How many spaces were left?

9. Mrs. Doyle intends to lay carpet for her bedroom which measures 4 m by 5 m. She visits a carpet shop which offers the following sale:

Carpet Sale!		
Regular	:	$9.90 per square meter
Now	:	20% off

How much will she need to pay for the carpet for her bedroom at this sale price?

10. Jerry read 140 pages of a story book on Saturday and 25% of the remaining pages on Sunday. If the book had 500 pages, what percentage of the book remained unread?

11. Sarah's house had a floor area of 100 m². A utility room measuring 5 m by 4 m was added. What was the percentage increase in the floor area of Sarah's house?

12. In December last year, Pauline's monthly salary was $1800. In January this year, her boss increased her salary by 8%. She placed the whole of her salary for January this year in a special one-year fixed deposit with a bank. The interest rate for this fixed deposit is 3% per year.
    (a) What was Pauline's salary in January this year?
    (b) How much money would she receive from the bank after 1 year? Give the answer correct to the nearest dollar.

13. 75% of the teachers in ABC Elementary School do not wear glasses. 10% of the total school population of 2640 are teachers.
    (a) What is the ratio of the number of teachers who wear glasses to the total number of teachers in the school?
    (b) How many teachers wear glasses?

14. A shopkeeper had 200 eggs. 5% of them were broken and thrown away. He sold $\frac{3}{5}$ of the remaining eggs and put the unsold eggs into 2 trays. If the bigger tray had 16 eggs more than the smaller tray, what percentage of the unsold eggs were put into the smaller tray? Give your answer correct to 1 decimal place.

15. Tim, Ken and Cindy collect baseball cards as their hobbies. Tim's collection is 75% of Ken's collection. Ken's collection is 80% of Cindy's collection. If Cindy throws 14 baseball cards away, she will have the same number of baseball cards as Tim.
    (a) What is the ratio of Cindy's collection to Ken's collection to Tim's collection?
    (b) How many times is Cindy's collection more than Tim's collection?
    (c) What is the total number of baseball cards collected by the three children?

Take the **Challenge!**

1. Consider these two cases:

    Case A: 3 students attempted all the multiple-choice questions in a test.
    The first student had 20% of the questions answered correctly.
    The second student had 30% of the questions answered correctly.
    The third student had 40% of the questions answered correctly.
    If the 3 students had answered a total of 45 questions correctly, the
    test consists of 50 questions.

    Case B: A journalist surveyed 20% of a group of 50 people and 80% of
    another group of 500 people.
    The journalist surveyed 50% of the total number of people.

    Which one of the two cases is wrong? Why?

2. Mr. Kit bought 2 Hello Kitty dolls for $50 each. Mr. Tee offered him $60 for
    one of the dolls and Mr. Kit sold it to him.
    Two days later, Mr. Kit bought back the same doll from Mr. Tee for $70. Mr.
    Kit subsequently sold it to another person for $80.
    However, Mr. Kit could not sell the other doll and he finally had to reduce its
    price to 10% below what he had paid for it.
    Did Mr. Kit make a profit or loss over the whole transaction?
    How much profit or loss did he make?

3. Macy expects her salary to increase yearly by 8% for the next 2 years. This year her annual salary is $30,000.

   She has been offered another job which will pay her $32,000 per year but her salary will remain the same for the next 2 years.

   Should Macy accept the new job offer? Why?

Topic 3: Average

1. Transfer the objects from one stick or container to another so that each stick or container will have equal number of objects.

(a)

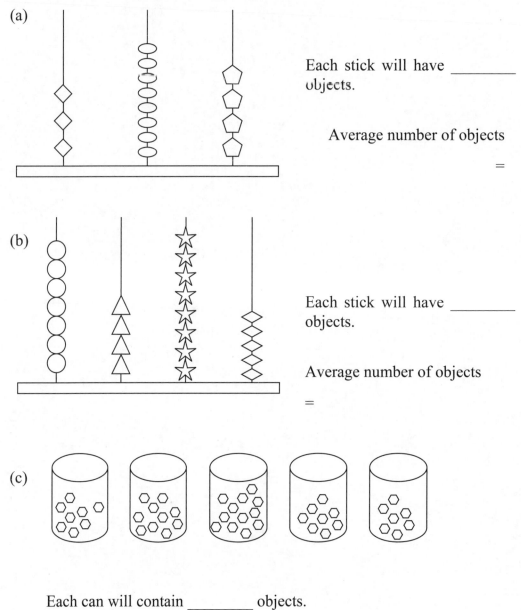

Each stick will have _____ objects.

Average number of objects

=

(b)

Each stick will have _____ objects.

Average number of objects

=

(c)

Each can will contain _____ objects.

Average number of objects = _____

2. Find the average of each set of numbers.

    (a) 82 and 64   _____   (b) 9, 13 and 17   _____

    (c) 11, 11, 11 and 11 _____   (d) 2, 7, 15 and 4   _____

    (e) 25 and 29   _____   (f) 32, 26 and 59   _____

3. The picture graph below shows the number of library books borrowed by five children in a week.

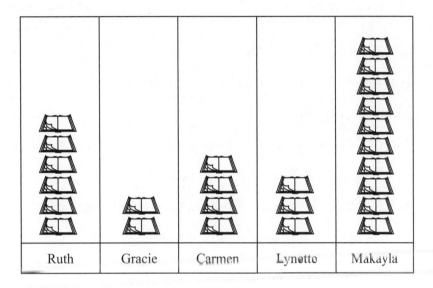

| | Ruth | Gracie | Carmen | Lynetto | Makayla |

    Average number of library books each child borrowed = _____

4. Find the average of each of the following.

    (a) $7.25, $1.75 and $6.60   _____

    (b) 99.5 kg and 101.5 kg   _____

    (c) 7.04 ℓ, 13.2 ℓ, 9.7 ℓ, 39.5 ℓ and 5.03 ℓ   _____

    (d) 1.59 m, 1.67 m, 1.81 m and 1.45 m   _____

    (e) 42.19 km, 100.16 km and 84.93 km   _____

5. Fill in the blanks.

    (a) The total height of a family of five is 7.65 m.

         Average height = _____

(b) 7 workers earn a total salary of $8323.

Average salary = _____

(c) 8 plastic bottles contain 16.24 gallons of water altogether.

Average amount of water = _____

(d) Sean, Alan, David, Irving and Charlie ran a total distance of 189.75 km in a marathon.

Average distance = _____

6 Fill in the blanks.

(a) Anne scored an average of 87.5 points for 4 subjects in an exam.

Total score for the 4 subjects = _____

(b) Mr. Lim gives his 3 daughters an average monthly allowance of $115.85.

Total monthly allowance for the 3 daughters = _____

(c) A seller cuts 300 pieces of rope at an average length of 95.5 cm.

Total length of the 300 pieces of rope = _____

(d) The average of the first 100 numbers is 50.5.

Sum of the 100 numbers = _____

7. Fill in the blanks.

(a) Average height of 4 girls is 4 ft 8 in.

Sum of their heights = _____ ft _____ in.

(b) Average volume of water in 3 buckets is 5 ℓ 425 ml.

Total volume of water = _____ ℓ _____ ml

(c) Average weight of 5 watermelons is 6 lb 8 oz.

Total weight = _____ lb _____ oz

(d) Average time taken to complete a puzzle individually by 9 children is 55 min.

Total time taken = _____ h _____ min

8. Fill in the blanks.

   (a) A car traveled a total distance of 150 km 584 m in 2 hours.

        Average distance = _____ km _____ m

   (b) It took 5 h 20 min to bake 4 cakes.

        Average time = _____ h _____ min

   (c) The total weight of 6 bags is 22 kg 200g.

        Average mass = _____ kg _____ g

   (d) The total volume of water in 7 containers is 141 qt 3 c.

        Average volume = _____ qt _____ c

9. The average of 5 consecutive numbers is 11. What is the largest of the
   5 numbers?
   (Consecutive numbers are numbers that follow one after another.)

10. Find the average of each of the following.

    (a) the first 5 consecutive numbers starting with 1   _____

    (b) the first 9 consecutive numbers starting with 1   _____

    (c) the first 7 consecutive even numbers starting with 2   _____

    (d) the first 5 consecutive odd numbers starting with 1   _____

    (e) the first 15 consecutive numbers starting with 1   _____

    (Can you predict the answers without working them out?)

11. Find the average of each of the following.

    (a) $\frac{1}{2}$ and $\frac{1}{3}$ _____   (b) $\frac{1}{2}$, $\frac{1}{3}$ and $\frac{1}{6}$ _____

12. Work out these problems.

    (a) The average of two numbers is 25. One number is less than the other
         number by 12. What are the two numbers?

35

(b)   The average height of 6 students is 1.56 m. The total height of 5 of them is 7.72 m. What is the height of the sixth student?

(c)   The average number of students in nine classes is 36. The number of students in each of these classes forms a set of consecutive numbers. What is the number of students in the smallest class?

(d)   There is an average of 462 trains arriving at a certain train station every month. If the station operates only 10 months in a year, what is the average number of trains arriving at the station in 9 years?

(e)   A dice is thrown 10 times. The results shown on the dice are as follows:

         3   5   1   2   6   4   2   5   3   1

What is the average result?

(f)   Six friends compare their scores for a history test. Their average score is 61. What is Christine's score?

Abby	Beatrice	Christine	Diana	Elsie	Faith
68	54	?	31	45	89

WORD PROBLEMS

1. Chris had 3 trial-runs for a race. His performance time for each trial-run was as follows:

1st trial-run	10 min 32 s
2nd trial-run	10 min 40 s
3rd trial-run	9 min 9 s

What was his average performance time?

2. For the past 4 math tests, Tessa scored an average of 78 points. She hopes to increase her average test score to 80 points. How many points must she get for the 5th math test?

3. A bookstore sold a total of 5400 books in the first year of operation. It sold 3960 books in the first 8 months of the year. What was the average number of books sold for the last 4 months of the year?

4. The average height of 8 ladies in a sports club is 1.59 m. Two of them are 1.60 m and 1.64 m tall. What is the average height of the other 6 ladies?

5. The average height of 4 boys is 152 cm and that of 5 girls is 149 cm. What is the average height of the 9 children? Give the answer in meters correct to 1 decimal place.

6. On the average, Diego and Mike each weighs $49\frac{1}{4}$ kg. If Mike is $2\frac{1}{2}$ kg heavier than Diego, how much does Diego weigh?

7. In a week, Ross spends a total of 4 h 40 min jogging.
   (a) Find the average time he spends jogging in a day.
   (b) If he maintains the same average jogging time, how much time does he spend jogging in 15 days? Give your answer in hours.

8. Eight colleagues went out for lunch together. The lunch cost $135.50. Bill paid $4.50 less than the average amount paid by the rest. How much did Bill pay?

9. Mr. Lim's average monthly utility bill for the first 6 months is $68. His average utility bill for the next 6 months of the year is $62 more than his average monthly utility bill for the first 6 months. Find Mr. Lim's average monthly utility bill for the whole year.

10. The table shows the donations received by a charity group during the first 5 days of a week.

Monday	Tuesday	Wednesday	Thursday	Friday
$540	$1063	$816	$1641	$2475

(a) Find the average donation received during the 5 days.

(b) More donations were received during the weekend. The average donation rose to $2675. How much money was received during the weekend?

11. In 1 hour, 15 machines can seal an average of 900 bottles. In 1 hour, 4 of the machines can seal an average of 800 bottles and 6 of the other machines can seal an average of 810 bottles. Find the average number of bottles the remaining machines can seal in 1 hour.

12. A group of children were surveyed on the number of pets they kept. The table below shows the results of the survey.

Number of Pets kept	0	1	2	3	4	5
Number of Children	3	8	10	14	6	9

(a) How many children took part in the survey?

(b) What was the total number of pets kept by the children?

(c) What was the average number of pets each child kept?
Round off the answer to the nearest whole number.

13. A carton can hold 16 bottles of milk. It weighs 750 g when it is empty and 15.15 kg when it is three-quarters full of bottles. On the average, how much does each bottle of milk weigh?

14. The average of two 3-digit numbers is 180. The first two digits of the first number are as shown.
What is the smallest possible number for the second number?

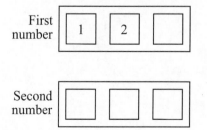

First number | 1 | 2 |

Second number | | |

15. A survey was conducted to find out the number of newspapers bought by some residents in a housing development during the past week. The results were shown in the bar graph below.

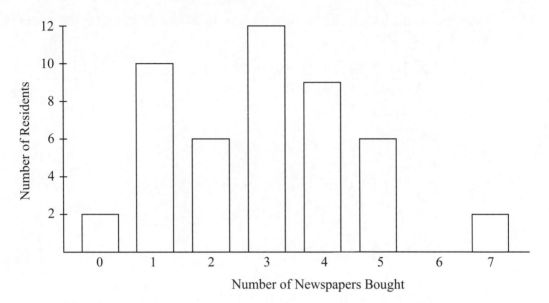

(a) How many residents were surveyed?

(b) What was the total number of newspapers bought by the residents during the week?

(c) What was the average number of newspapers the residents bought? (Give the answer correct to the nearest whole number.)

Take the Challenge!

1. Find the sum of each of the following sets of numbers using the concept of average.

   (a) $1 + 2 + 3 + 4 + \ldots + 27 + 28 + 29 + 30$

   (b) $13 + 15 + 17 + 19 + \ldots + 93 + 95 + 97 + 99$

   (c) $18 + 22 + 26 + 30 + \ldots + 118 + 122 + 126 + 130$

2. Aunt Norleena saw two advertisements for sewing machine operators.

Sewing Machine Operators
Next Fashion, requires female sewing machine operators. Conducive working environment. Normal shift, 5 days a week. Average wage for employees is over $300 per week.   Contact our Personnel Officer to arrange for an interview.

Top Clothes
requires: sewing machine operators   Good conditions and pay. Transport provided. Most of our employees earn at least $300 per week.   Come for a walk-in interview.

The table below shows the actual wages paid to 100 employees in each company. Study it and answer the following questions.

Company	Next Fashion				Top Clothes			
Weekly Wage ($)	200	250	400	1800	200	250	300	600
Number of employees earning this wage	40	32	24	4	10	40	45	5

(a)   Complete the bar graph below with the data from the table.

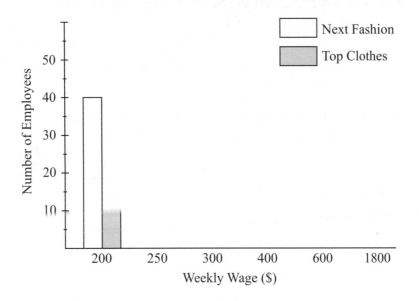

(b)   What is the average weekly wage of the 100 employees in Next Fashion company?

(c)   What is the average weekly wage of the 100 employees in Top Clothes company?

(d) In Next Fashion, what weekly wage do most of the employees earn?

(e) In Top Clothes, how much do most of the employees make in a week?

(f) Did both advertisements provide the true information?

(g) Which company do you think Aunt Norleena should work with? Why?

Topic 4: Rate

1. Solve the following.

(a) Mr. Morris bought 24 jugs of 1-gallon milk. Mr. Morris and his family finished the milk in 4 weeks. If they drank the same amount of milk each week, how many gallons of milk did they drink every week?

_____ gallons

(b) The table shows the rates of charges for making telephone calls to Canada.

Standard Rate (7 am to 6:59 pm)	Economy Rate (7 pm to 6:59 am)
50 seconds call duration for every 10 cents	67 seconds call duration for every 10 cents

At which of the following times of a day would you make a half-hour telephone call to Canada which would cost you the least money?

Circle the answer.

| 3:30 am | | 7:15 am | | 6:50 pm |

(c) One man will take one day to dig a hole which is 2 m long, 2 m wide and 2 m deep. If 2 other men come along to help dig the same hole, will the three men still take 1 day to complete the job if they work together at the same pace?

_____

How long will the 3 men take to complete the job?
Circle the answer.

| 1 day | | $\frac{1}{3}$ day | | $\frac{1}{2}$ day |

2. Find the rate for each of the following.
   Work out how much/many of one quantity for every unit value of the other quantity.

   (a) I save $24 in 3 months.

   Rate = $24 ÷ 3 = $_____ per month

   (b) Ruth speed reads 12,000 words in 20 minutes.

   Rate = _____ words per minute

   (c) ABC Factory manufactures 35,000 transistor radios in 7 days.

   Rate = _____ transistor radios per day

   (d) A certain car traveled 180 km on 12 liters of gas.

   Rate = _____ km per liter of gas

   (e) Wheel A turns 96 rounds as wheel B turns 128 rounds.

   Rate = _____ turns of wheel B per turn of wheel A

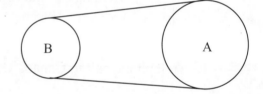

   (f) A contractor quoted a price of $6960 to lay ceramic floor tiles for a floor area of 120 m².

   Rate = $_____ per m²

   (g) Roslan completed a 41.85 km race in $4\frac{1}{2}$ hours.

   Rate = _____ m per min

3. Based on the given rate, work out each of the following.

   (a) Tom rents a car at $55 per day.

   Total cost of renting a car for 5 days = $_____

(b)   A machine produces 15 plastic bags per minute.

    Number of plastic bags produced in 25 minutes = _____

(c)   Ted paid monthly installments of $465 for 2 years.

    Total amount paid = $_____

(d)   Water leaks from a tank at the rate of 0.5 liters per minute.

    Volume of water leaked in $2\frac{1}{2}$ hours = _____ liters

(e)   Prawns were sold at $1.99 per 100 g.

    Cost of 3 kg of prawns = $_____

(f)   I read a novel in $3\frac{2}{3}$ hours.

    Time taken to read 4 such novels = _____ hours

(g)   Lynette jogged at a pace of 2.5 meters per second.

    Distance jogged in $1\frac{1}{4}$ hours = _____ km

(h)   A laborer is paid a rate of $4.50 per hour.

    Amount of money earned for working 28 days at 10 hours a day
    = $_____

(i)   2 worms provide 0.5 g of protein.

    Amount of protein 100 worms provide = _____ g

4. Work out the following using the concept of proportion.

    Example:
        A machine makes 400 bags in 40 minutes.
        How many bags can it make in 25 minutes?

    Solution:
        It makes (400 ÷ 8) bags in (40 ÷ 8) mins = 50 bags in 5 minutes
        It makes (50 × 5) bags in (5 × 5) mins = **250 bags** in 25 minutes

(a) In a year, Abby saved $2700. If she saved the same amount of money every month, how much was her savings for 3 months?

(b) A ream of paper has a thickness of 5.4 cm. If there are 500 sheets of paper in the ream of paper, what is the thickness of 100 sheets of paper?

(c) Juliana can type 2400 words in $\frac{2}{5}$ h. If she types at the same rate, how many words can she type in 15 minutes?

(d) Naomi can make 75 ribbons in 30 minutes. At this rate, how long does she take to make 120 similar ribbons?

(e) If 140 scarves can be cut from 4 meters of cloth, how many scarves of the same size can be cut from 9 meters of the same type of cloth?

(f) Each wheel of a car covers a distance of 30 m when it makes 8 revolutions. At this rate, what distance will each wheel cover when it makes 12 revolutions?
(A revolution is a complete turn.)

(g) Melissa deposits an equal amount of savings in her bank each month. If she saves $912 in 6 months, how much savings will she have in $2\frac{1}{6}$ years?

(h)   4 bags of flour cost \$5.20. How much money must Mrs. Perry pay for 2 dozen bags of flour?

(i)   If a family consumes 800 g of rice every 2 days, how many days will they take to finish a 6-kg bag of rice?

(j)   My car can travel 18 mi on a gallon of gas. If the gas costs \$1.20 per gallon, what is the cost of gas for traveling 180 mi?

(k)   It costs \$2 to paint 25 cm of a flag pole. Find the cost of painting $8\frac{3}{4}$ m of a similar flag pole.

(l)   If 9 workers take 10 hours to complete a piece of job, how long will 8 workers take to complete the same piece of job?

(m)   It takes Aaron 20 hours to paint a house. It takes Bob 30 hours to paint the same house. How long do both of them take if they work together to paint the same house?

(n)   One man alone takes one day to dig a hole which is 2 m long, 2 m wide and 2 m deep. How long do 3 men take to dig a hole which is 4 m long, 4 m wide and 4 m deep if they work together at the same pace?

5. The following table shows the yearly road tax payable for different categories of cars.

Category of Car by Size	Road Tax Charges
Below 1000 cc	$0.45 per cc
1000 cc to 1599 cc	$0.56 per cc
1600 cc to 1999 cc	$0.69 per cc
2000 cc and above	$1.03 per cc

Note: 'cc' stands for cm^3

(a) Louise drives a 998 cc car. How much road tax does she have to pay for half a year?

(b) Maury owns a 2000 cc car. How much road tax does he have to pay every year?

6. The table below shows the rates of charges for bus fare of a certain transport company.

First one half mile	60 cents
Every additional quarter mile	10 cents

(a) Julie boarded a bus for a $1\frac{1}{2}$ mile trip from her school to her house. How much did she pay for her bus fare?

(b) Mrs. Tan travels by bus to the store every morning. The bus trip between her home and the store is 4 miles. How much bus fare does she pay to do her shopping every day, assuming that the bus travels the same journey to and fro?

7. The parking fee for cars in the basement parking lot of a shopping center is given below.

Daily Parking Rates from 7:30 am to 10:00 pm	
1st hour or part thereof	$3.50
Every additional half hour or part thereof	$1.50
After 5:00 pm	$2.50 per entry

(a) Simon parked his car in the parking lot from 10:30 am to 1:00 pm. How much parking fee did he pay?

(b) Dr. De Souza owns a clinic in the shopping center. She parks her car in the parking lot daily from 9:30 am to 9:00 pm, except on Saturdays and Sundays. What is her daily parking charges?

8. The table shows the postage rates for the delivery of mail to a certain country.

Weight not more than	Postage charge in cents
20 g	30
50 g	40
100 g	70
Every additional 100 g or less	60

(a) Find the postage for a magazine which weighs 95 g.

(b) I want to send a 'health' magazine which weighs about 850 g to my friend in that country. How much postage do I need to pay?

WORD PROBLEMS

1. A hall is 100 yards long by 30.5 yards wide. What is the cost of tiling the floor at a rate of $2.50 per square yard?

2. Donald's pace of walking is 7 strides in 10 seconds. If his average stride is 63 cm, how far can he walk in one minute?

3. 1.35 m of cloth is needed to sew a pair of pants and 1.6 m of cloth is needed to sew a shirt. How many meters of cloth does a tailor need if he wants to sew 8 pairs of pants and 8 shirts altogether?

4. At a supermarket, plums are sold at 5 for $2.85 and kiwi fruits at 3 for $1.20. How much does Mrs. Lee need to pay for 15 kiwi fruits and 20 plums?

5. A plumber is paid $10 an hour for normal working hours from 9 am to 5 pm. He is paid $1\frac{1}{2}$ times his normal hourly wage when he works overtime. How much does he earn for working 12 hours on a certain day?

6. The postage rates for sending packages to a certain country are as follows:

For the first 200 g	$5.50
For every additional 150 g	$2.30

Find the postage for a package weighing 1.3 kg.

7. The room rates at a local resort hotel are as follows:

Room type	Weekday	Weekend (Sat & Sun)
Deluxe room (Queen-sharing)	$180	$210
Executive Suite (Queen-sharing)	$260	$290
Extra bed	$35	$35

Mr. and Mrs. Sheridan want to book a deluxe room in the hotel from Thursday to Sunday of the same week. They will be bringing their nine-year-old son for the stay in the hotel. How much do they need to pay for the accommodation?

8. John wants to buy 6 liters of guava-pineapple juice. In a grocery store, he found that the juice is sold either in 750-ml cans at $4.65 per can, or in 1-liter bottles at $5.85 per bottle. Should John buy the juice in cans or in bottles? Why?

9. The rates of charges for taxi fare are as follows :

For the first km or part thereof	$2.40
For every half km or part thereof	$0.40

Cecilia paid $10.80 for taxi fare to travel from her home to her office. What is the distance between her home and office?

10. A bricklayer can lay 36 bricks in an hour. He needs to build 3 walls to form an extra room for a house. If each wall requires 350 bricks to build, how long will the bricklayer take to finish the job? Give the answer in hours and minutes.

11. A tank can hold 180 gallons of water when it is full. Water flows from 2 small pipes and 1 large pipe into the empty tank at the same time. Each small pipe can fill the tank at a rate of 6 gallons of water per minute while the large pipe fills the tank at a rate of 8 gallons per minute. How long does it take the 3 pipes to fill the tank to the brim?

12. A worker in a factory is paid the following wages.

Working hours	Hourly wage
Normal: 8:00 am to 5:00 pm	$4.80
Overtime: 5:00 pm to 7:00 pm	$1\frac{1}{2}$ times normal hourly wage
Overtime: Beyond 7:00 pm	2 times normal hourly wage

On a certain day, he was paid $43.20 for working overtime. How many hours did he work altogether on that day?

13. In a factory, machine A can produce 230 fortune cookies in 5 minutes, while machine B can produce 20 more fortune cookies in the same 5 minutes. The factory receives an order for 4800 fortune cookies.

(a) How long does it take both machines to produce the 4800 fortune cookies, assuming the 2 machines are operating together continuously?

(b) What is the total time taken to produce the 4800 fortune cookies if machine A breaks down after operating for 45 minutes? Give the answer in minutes and seconds.

14. A 1.6-m deep swimming pool has been emptied and cleaned. After the cleaning, water is pumped into the pool. The water level increases at a rate of 6.5 cm in every 2 minutes. However, water also drains away at a rate of 0.25 cm in every 5 minutes.
   (a) How long will it take to fill the pool?

   (b) What is the water level in the pool after $\frac{2}{3}$ h?

Take the Challenge!

1. In a particular year, a study found that cars burn off 6% of gasoline during traffic jams.

   (a) If a car uses 1850 gallons of gasoline per year, how many gallons of gasoline are lost by the car per month during traffic jams in that year?

   (b) The average price of gasoline in that year was $1.20 per gallon. How much money in total did it cost the car owners that year in terms of gasoline wastage during traffic jams, if there were 100,000 cars then?

2. 4 people can catch 6 fish in 30 minutes. How many people are needed to catch 18 fish in 3 hours?

3. Tap A alone can fill a tank in 3 minutes. Tap B alone can fill the same tank in 4 minutes. When the 2 taps are turned on at the same time, how long will it take the two taps to fill the tank completely?

4. Faith and Gail are given two projects to do.
    Faith needs 10 days to complete Project Alpha and 15 days to complete Project Beta.
    Gail needs 8 days to complete Project Alpha and 20 days to complete Project Beta.
    The two girls decide to team up to complete the 2 projects in the shortest possible time.
    What is the least number of hours they will take to complete both projects, working independently and collaboratively?

Topic 5: Graphs

1. As part of a math lesson on graphs, a fifth grade class was asked to do a survey on the type of vehicles that passed by their school gate one morning. A group of students recorded their survey results in the table below.

Type of Vehicle	Number of Vehicles
Motorcycles	10
Pickups	15
Cars	60
Buses	25
Trucks	10

Complete the bar graph below to show the results of the survey.

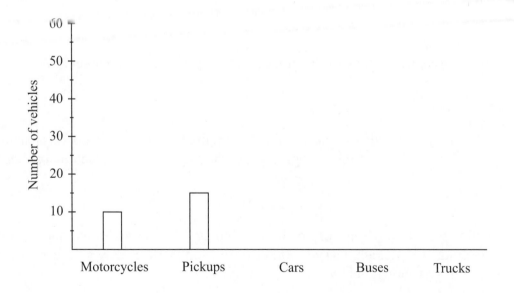

2. A survey was carried out on a group of 1000 graduates who graduated last year to find out their occupations.

Study the bar graph, which shows the results of the survey and answer the questions that follow.

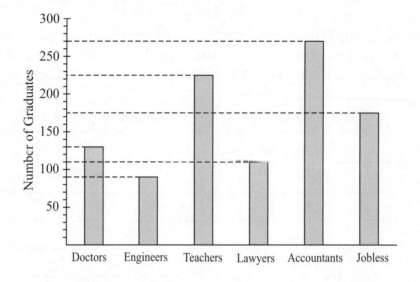

(a) What fraction of the graduates were still without a job at the time the survey was taken?

(b) What percentage of the graduates took up a teaching career?

(c) Find the ratio of the number of graduates who took up the teaching career to the number of graduates who took up a non-teaching career.

3. Chloe grew a seedling in a small pot at home. She measured the height of the seedling at 9 o'clock every morning from Monday to Friday and recorded the readings as shown below.

Monday	Tuesday	Wednesday	Thursday	Friday
2 cm	3 cm	6 cm	9 cm	14 cm

(a) Complete the line graph to show the growth of the seedling and answer the questions that follow.

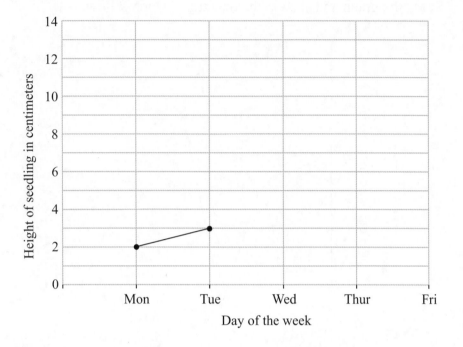

(b) What was the height of the seedling on Wednesday as a fraction of its height on Friday?

(c) How much did the seedling grow in the five days?

(d) Between which two days did the seedling grow the most? What was the increase in the height?

(e) Between which days did the seedling grow at the same rate? What was the rate during this period, in cm per day?

4. The line graph shows the number of readers for a popular women's magazine during the first six months of the year.
Study the graph and answer the questions which follow.

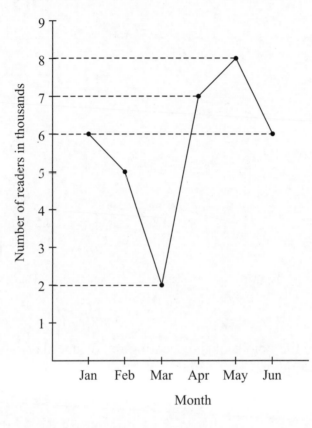

(a) What was the total number of readers for the women's magazine in the first 3 months?

(b) What was the increase in readership from March to May?

(c) In which month was the highest increase in readership recorded?

(d) In which month was the largest drop in readership recorded?

(e) What was the average number of readers for the first six months of the year? Give the answer correct to the nearest hundred readers.

5. The table below shows some of the points scored by 4 students in an exam.

(a) Using the information given, fill in the missing points for the other subjects in the table.

Rennie's points for math was the average of the math score of Megan, Natalie and Leela.

The ratio of Megan's points to Natalie's points to Leela's points for math was 7 : 10 : 9.

The total points scored by Megan and Natalie for science was 144.

Megan scored 20 points more than Natalie in science.

The total science points scored by Leela and Rennie was 10 points more than the total science points scored by Megan and Natalie.

Leela scored 30 points more than Rennie for science.

Subject / Name	Science	English	Mathematics	Total Score
Megan		71		
Natalie		81		
Leela		91		
Rennie		86	78	

(b) Which subject did Rennie score the lowest? _____

(c) Who scored the highest in math? _____

(d) Who scored the lowest total score for all the 3 subjects? _____

(e) If you were to show the overall performance of the 4 students using a graph, which type of graph would you choose, a bar graph or a line graph? Why?

6. The line graph tracks the monthly sales at a shop in a shopping mall from June to December last year. Study the graph and answer the questions which follow.

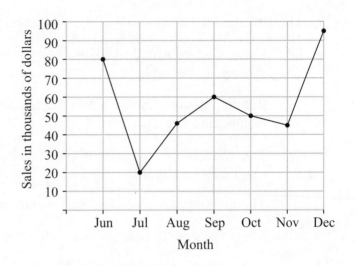

(a) What is the difference in sales between the months of June and December?

(b) Can you explain the higher sales during December, compared to the sales in the other months?

(c) Between which two months is there a 75% reduction in sales?

(d) If the shop owner wants to close his shop to go for a holiday, in which month should he choose to go for a holiday?

(e) What is the percentage increase in sales in December as compared to the sales in June?

7. The line graphs below show the temperatures of two cities, Mayberry and Lake Woebegon, in a particular week during the month of November. Study the graphs and answer the questions which follow.

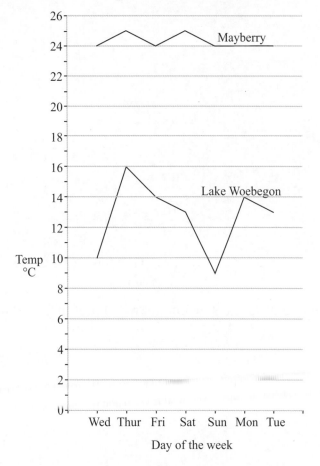

(a) On which day was the difference in temperature between Mayberry and Lake Woebegon the largest?

(b) On which day did both cities experience their highest temperature for that week? What was the difference in temperature between the 2 cities on that day?

(c) What does the steepness of the line graph of Lake Woebegon tell you about the temperature changes between Wednesday and Thursday; and between Sunday and Monday?

8. The amount of rainfall in 2 cities, M and P, over a period of one week were charted in the line graphs below. Study the graphs and answer the questions which follow.

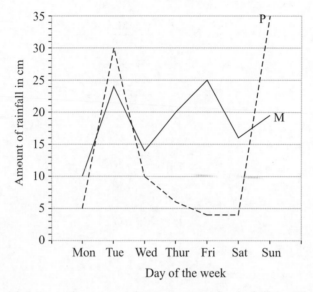

(a) On which two days was the amount of rainfall in City P the same?

(b) On which days was the amount of rainfall in City P more than that in City M?

(c) What was the difference between the average amount of rainfall from Monday to Wednesday in City M and that in City P?

(d) What can you tell about the change in the amount of rainfall between Wednesday and Friday in City P and that in City M?

(e) What was the difference in the total amount of rainfall between the 2 cities for the week?

1. A country's grape produce (in millions of kg) for the years 1950, 1960, 1970, 1980, 1990 and 2000 is represented by a line graph as shown .
Use the graph to answer the questions which follow.

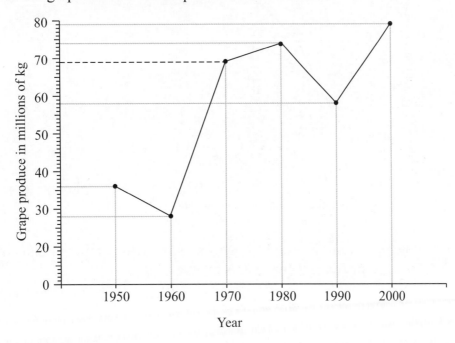

(a) What was the decrease in grape produce in this country in the year 1990 compared to that in 1980?

(b) What was the country's average grape produce from 1950 to 2000?

(c) In 1970, 80% of the grape produce were exported. How many kilograms of grape produce were consumed in the country that year?

(d) Does the graph give you any indication of the grape produce between the years 1960 and 1970 or between the years 1980 and 1990?

(e) Estimate the amount of grape produce in 1965 and in 1985.

2. The line graph shows the production of jeans in a certain factory that employs sewing machine operators.
   Study the graph and answer the questions that follow.

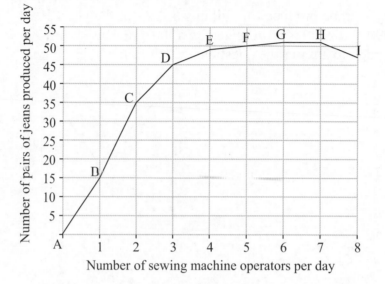

(a) Which point on the graph shows the maximum number of pairs of jeans produced per day? What is this rate?

(b) At least how many sewing machine operators are needed to reach the maximum production of jeans per day?

(c) The wage of a sewing machine operator is $80 per day and the cost of running each sewing machine is $20 per day. What is the cost of producing 1 pair of jeans when 6 operators are employed? Give the answer to the nearest dollar.

(d) Would you consider hiring more than 6 workers to increase production of jeans? Explain your answer.

Topic 6: Triangles

1. The sum of the three angles in a triangle is 180°. Find the unknown angle x in each of the following triangles which are not drawn to scale.

(a)

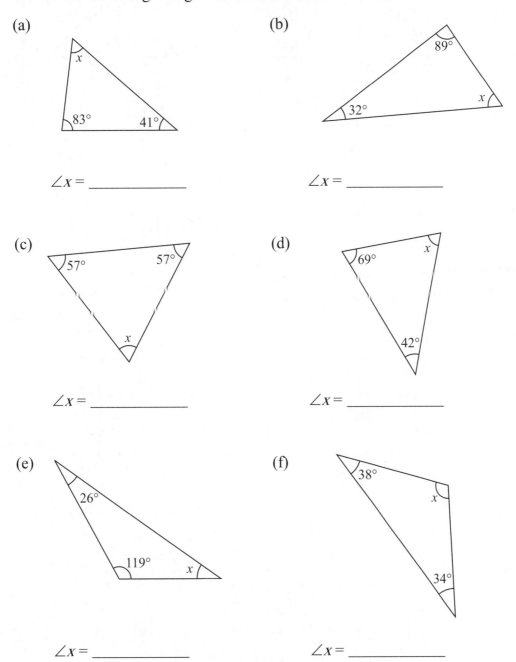

∠x = _____

(b)

∠x = _____

(c)

∠x = _____

(d)

∠x = _____

(e)

∠x = _____

(f)

∠x = _____

2. In a right-angled triangle, there is a right angle and two other angles which add up to 90°. Using this property of a right-angled triangle, identify each right-angled triangle by putting a check (✔) in the box given.

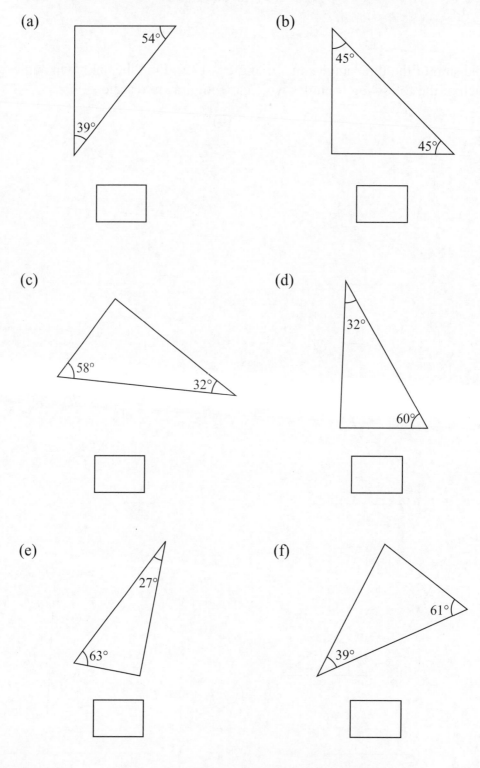

(a)

54°

39°

(b)

45°

45°

(c)

58°

32°

(d)

32°

60°

(e)

27°

63°

(f)

61°

39°

3. Using the same property of a right-angled triangle as stated in Question 2, find the value of the unknown angle y in each of the following triangles.

(a)

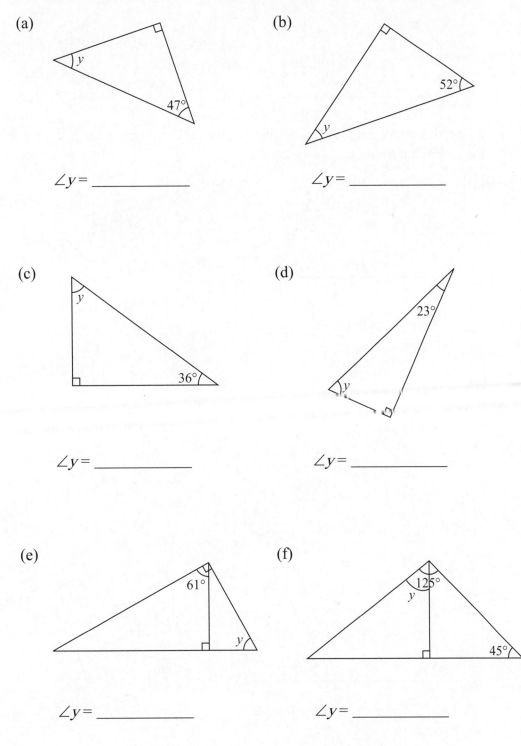

$\angle y =$ _____

(b)

$\angle y =$ _____

(c)

$\angle y =$ _____

(d)

$\angle y =$ _____

(e)

$\angle y =$ _____

(f)

$\angle y =$ _____

4. When one side of a triangle is extended, the exterior angle formed is equal to the sum of the two interior opposite angles as shown below.

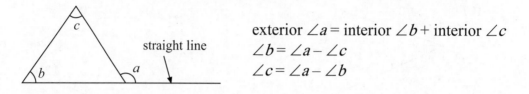

exterior $\angle a$ = interior $\angle b$ + interior $\angle c$

$\angle b = \angle a - \angle c$

$\angle c = \angle a - \angle b$

Using the above property, find the value of the unknown angle z in each of the following triangles.

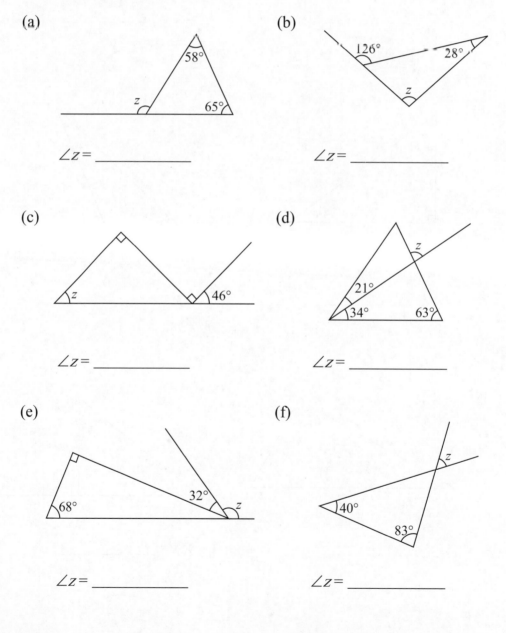

(a)

58°

z 65°

$\angle z =$ _____

(b)

126°   28°

z

$\angle z =$ _____

(c)

z 46°

$\angle z =$ _____

(d)

z

21°

34°   63°

$\angle z =$ _____

(e)

68°   32° z

$\angle z =$ _____

(f)

z

40°

83°

$\angle z =$ _____

70

5. In an isosceles triangle, two sides of the triangle are equal and they each form an equal base angle with the third side.
An isosceles triangle:

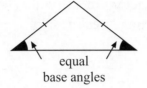

equal
base angles

Using a ruler or a protractor, identify the isosceles triangles from the following triangles by circling 'Yes' or 'No'.
Mark the equal sides of each isosceles triangle and measure the size of its base angle.

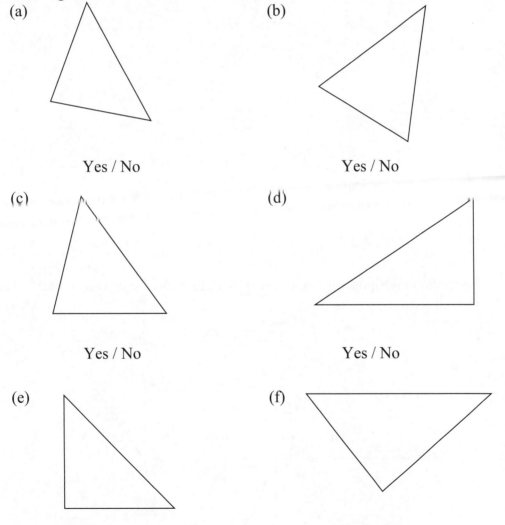

(a)

Yes / No

(b)

Yes / No

(c)

Yes / No

(d)

Yes / No

(e)

Yes / No

(f)

Yes / No

6. An equilateral triangle has 3 equal sides and 3 equal angles.
    Each angle = 180° ÷ 3
                = 60°

    Using a ruler or a protractor, identify the equilateral triangles from the following triangles by circling 'Yes' or 'No'.

    (a)   (b)

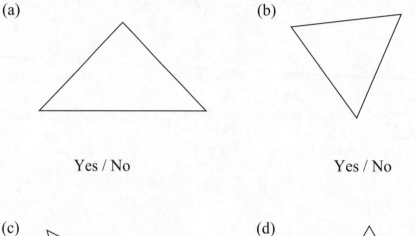

            Yes / No   Yes / No

    (c)   (d)

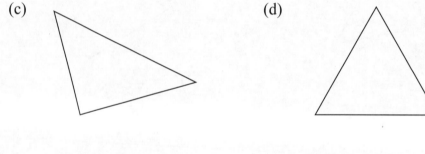

            Yes / No   Yes / No

7. The following figures are not drawn to scale. Find the unknown marked angle in each figure.

    (a)   (b)

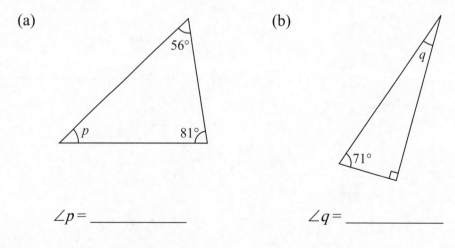

        ∠p = _____   ∠q = _____

(c)

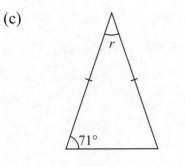

$\angle r =$ _____

(d)

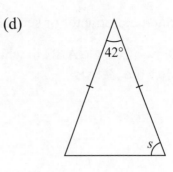

$\angle s =$ _____

(e)

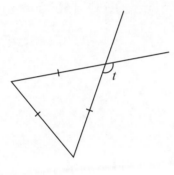

$\angle t =$ _____

(f)

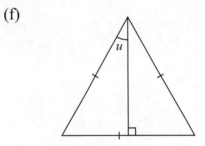

$\angle u =$ _____

(g)

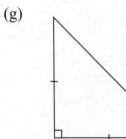

$\angle v =$ _____

(h)

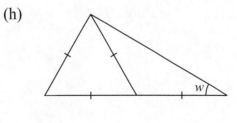

$\angle w =$ _____

8. Use a ruler, a protractor or set-square to construct the following triangles.

    (a) Draw a triangle ABC in which AB = 6 cm, BC = 4 cm and ∠ABC = 70°. Measure ∠CAB.

    A   B

    (b) Draw a triangle PQR in which PQ = 7 cm, ∠RPQ = 50° and ∠PQR = 45°. Measure the length of side PR.

    (c) Draw a triangle STR in which ST = 6 cm, TR = 9 cm and ∠RST = 120°. Measure ∠STR.

WORD PROBLEMS

1. In the figure, not drawn to scale, AC is a straight line and BCD is an equilateral triangle. Find $\angle a$.

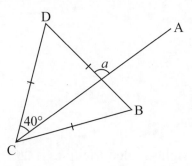

2. In the figure, not drawn to scale, AB and AC are straight lines. Find $\angle b$.

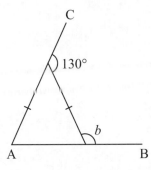

3. The figure, not drawn to scale, is made up of two triangles. Find $\angle c$.

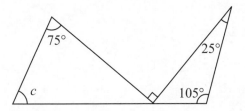

75

4. The figure, not drawn to scale, is made up of a square and 3 different triangles. Find ∠*d*.

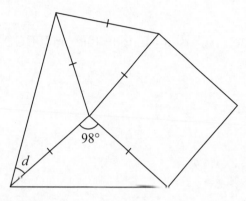

5. In the figure, not drawn to scale, PQR is a right-angled triangle. If ∠PSQ = 107° and PQ = QR, find ∠SQR.

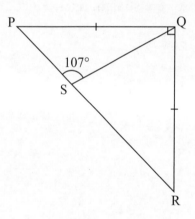

6. In the figure, not drawn to scale, BCE is a straight line. Find ∠DCE.

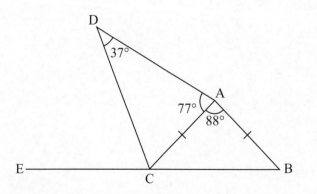

7. The figure, not drawn to scale, is made up of a rectangle, a triangle, and two lines. Find ∠e in the figure.

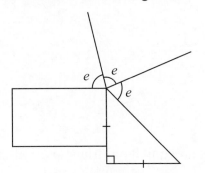

8. The figure, not drawn to scale, shows an isosceles triangle ADE inside triangle ACD. Find the sum of ∠CAE and ∠CDE.

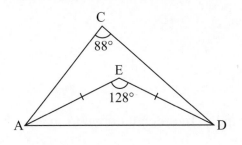

9. In the figure, not drawn to scale, PRST is a straight line. OR = PR and OS = ST. Find ∠POT.

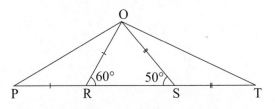

10. The figure, not drawn to scale, shows two overlapping triangles with BE = DE, ∠CAB = 32° and ∠EFC = 48°. Find ∠BED.

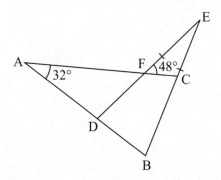

11. The figure, not drawn to scale, is formed by triangle ABC and triangle ADC. ∠BAD = ∠CAD and ∠ACD = ∠BCD. Find ∠ADC.

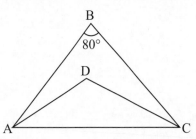

12. In the figure, not drawn to scale, DEF is an equilateral triangle. Find the sum of the angles *a*, *b*, *c* and *d*.

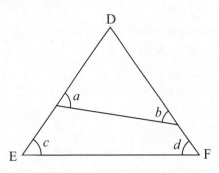

13. Find the sum of ∠*p*, ∠*q*, ∠*r* and ∠*s* in the figure, not drawn to scale.

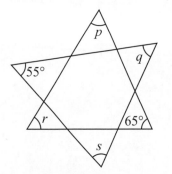

14. In the figure, not drawn to scale, RS is perpendicular to PQ and RT is a straight line. Fill in the missing angle in the statement below.

∠*a* + ∠*b* = ∠_____ + ∠g

15. In the figure, PQR is a straight line. Fill in the missing angle in the statement below.

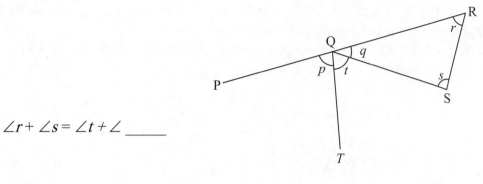

$\angle r + \angle s = \angle t + \angle$ _____

Take the Challenge!

1. Study the figure below carefully. ABC and ADE are isosceles triangles in which AB = AC and AD = AE. Given that $\angle BAD = 30°$, find $\angle x$.

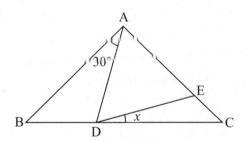

2. The pentagon (five-sided figure) below is formed with 5 identical isosceles triangles. One of its sides is extended to form a straight line XYZ. Find $\angle x$.

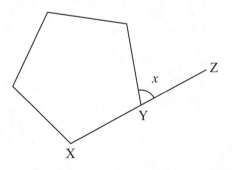

3. Look at the two triangles above.
   The L-shaped and triangular pieces in both figures seem to be identical in size but why do the pieces in the figure on the right not occupy the whole figure the way the pieces occupy the figure on the left?
   Explain why there is an empty space in the middle of the figure on the right.
   (*Hint:* Examine with a ruler.)

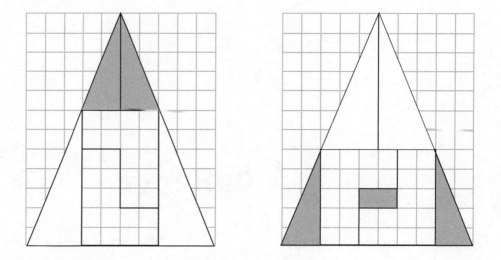

4. Figure A is made up of 2 isosceles triangles. Five such shapes are arranged to form a star in a pentagon (5-sided figure) as shown in Figure B. Find ∠p.

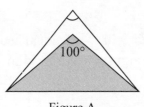

Figure A

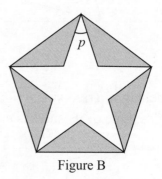

Figure B

Topic 7: 4-sided Figures

1. Fill in the blanks.

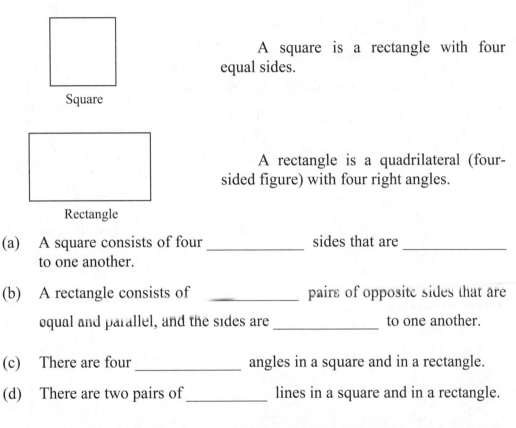

Square

A square is a rectangle with four equal sides.

Rectangle

A rectangle is a quadrilateral (four-sided figure) with four right angles.

(a) A square consists of four _____ sides that are _____ to one another.

(b) A rectangle consists of _____ pairs of opposite sides that are equal and parallel, and the sides are _____ to one another.

(c) There are four _____ angles in a square and in a rectangle.

(d) There are two pairs of _____ lines in a square and in a rectangle.

2. Are the following true about a parallelogram? Write 'T' (true) or 'F' (false) in the parentheses accordingly.

A parallelogram is a quadrilateral with each pair of the opposite sides parallel.

Parallelogram

(a) 2 opposite sides are equal. (   )

(b) All the four sides must be equal. (   )

(c) 2 pairs of parallel lines (   )

(d)   Only 1 pair of parallel lines   (   )

(e)   No parallel lines   (   )

(f)   Must not have any right angle   (   )

(g)   Must have 2 right angles   (   )

(h)   May have 4 right angles   (   )

(i)   Opposite angles are equal.   (   )

(j)   Adjacent angles are equal.   (   )

(k)   Sum of 2 adjacent angles is 180°.   (   )

(l)   Always has 2 isosceles triangles   (   )

3. Are the following true about a rhombus? Write 'T' (true) or 'F' (false) in the
    parentheses accordingly.

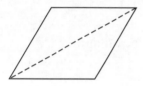

Rhombus

A rhombus is a quadrilateral with four
equal sides.

(a)   2 opposite sides are equal.   (   )

(b)   All the four sides must be equal.   (   )

(c)   2 pairs of parallel lines   (   )

(d)   Only 1 pair of parallel lines   (   )

(e)   No parallel lines   (   )

(f)   Must not have any right angle   (   )

(g)   Must have 2 right angles   (   )

(h)   May have 4 right angles   (   )

(i)   Opposite angles are equal.   (   )

(j)   Adjacent angles are equal.   (   )

(k)   Sum of 2 adjacent angles is 180°.   (   )

(l)   Always has at least two isosceles triangles   (   )

4. Are the following true about a trapezoid? Write 'T' (true) or 'F' (false) in the parentheses accordingly.

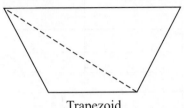

Trapezoid

A trapezoid is a quadrilateral with one pair of parallel lines.

(a)　2 opposite sides are always equal.　　　　　　　(　)

(b)　All the four sides must be equal.　　　　　　　(　)

(c)　Must have 2 pairs of parallel lines　　　　　　(　)

(d)　Have at least 1 pair of parallel lines　　　　　(　)

(e)　No parallel lines　　　　　　　　　　　　　(　)

(f)　Must not have any right angle　　　　　　　　(　)

(g)　Must have 2 right angles　　　　　　　　　　(　)

(h)　May have 4 right angles　　　　　　　　　　(　)

(i)　Opposite angles are always equal.　　　　　　(　)

(j)　Adjacent angles are always equal.　　　　　　(　)

(k)　Sum of 2 adjacent angles is always 180°.　　　(　)

(l)　Always has 2 isosceles triangles　　　　　　　(　)

5. Look at each of the following 4-sided figures. Identify each figure if it is a parallelogram, a rhombus or a trapezoid using a ruler and a set-square. Fill in the table on the next page with 'Yes' or 'No' accordingly. The first row of the table has been filled in.

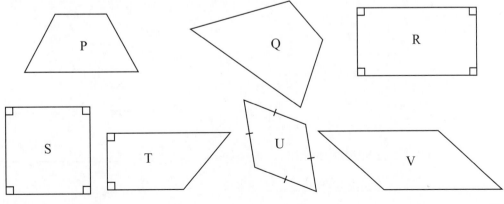

83

	4-sided figure	Parallelogram	Trapezoid	Rhombus
(a)	P	No	Yes	No
(b)	Q			
(c)	R			
(d)	S			
(e)	T			
(f)	U			
(g)	V			

6. Are the following statements true? Circle the correct answer.

(a) All parallelograms are squares.   Yes / No

(b) All parallelograms are rhombuses.   Yes / No

(c) All parallelograms are rectangles.   Yes / No

(d) A square is a rhombus with 4 right angles.   Yes / No

(e) A rhombus is a parallelogram.   Yes / No

(f) When the 4 angles in a parallelogram are right angles,   Yes / No
     it can be a rectangle.

(g) When the 4 angles in a parallelogram are right angles   Yes / No
     and all the sides are of equal length, it is a square.

7. Study the diagrams carefully. Can you figure out which type of 4-sided figures and how many of each type make up each diagram? Write the number of shapes in the parentheses and the names of the 4-sided figures in the blanks provided. Draw lines on the diagrams to show the 4-sided figures that are identified. The first one has been done for you.

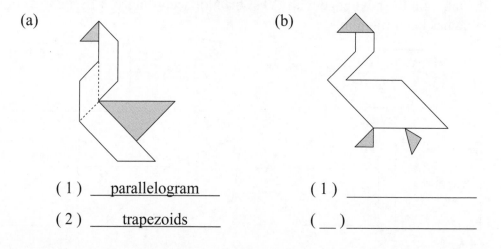

(a)

(b)

(1) ___parallelogram___   (1) _____

(2) ___trapezoids___   (_)_____

84

(c)

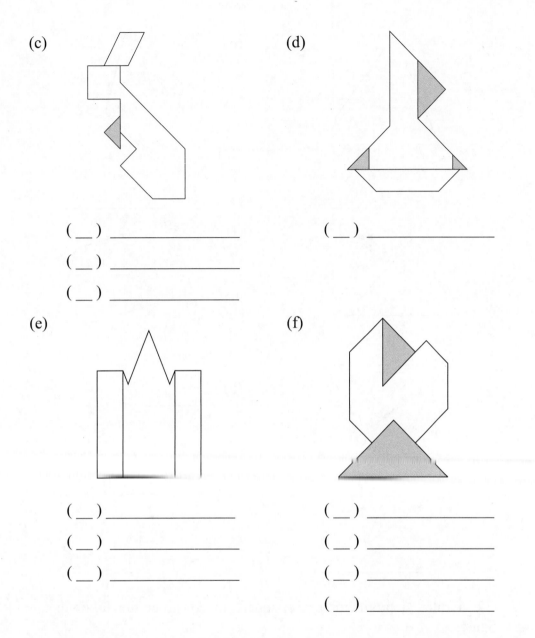

(_) _____

(_) _____

(_) _____

(d)

(_) _____

(e)

(_) _____

(_) _____

(_) _____

(f)

(_) _____

(_) _____

(_) _____

(_) _____

8. Find the unknown marked angle in each of the following figures, not drawn to scale.

(a)

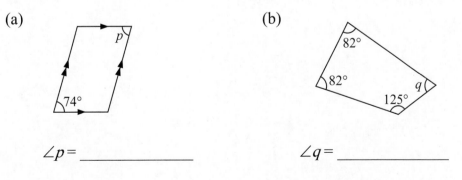

74°

∠p = _____

(b)

82°

82°

125° q

∠q = _____

85

(c)

(d)

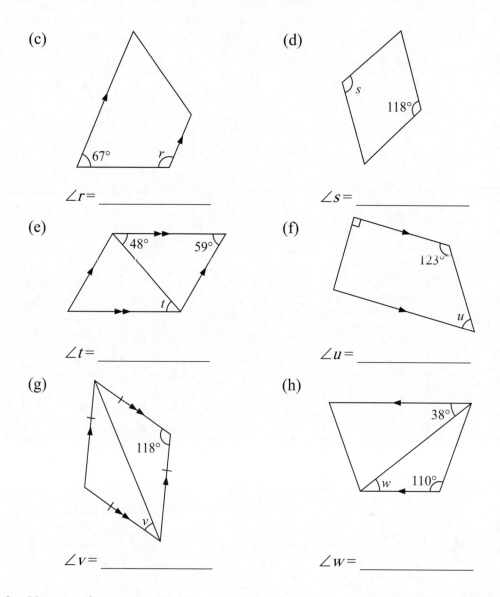

∠r = _____

∠s = _____

(e)

48°   59°

t

(f)

123°

u

∠t = _____

∠u = _____

(g)

118°

v

(h)

38°

w   110°

∠v = _____

∠w = _____

9. Use a ruler, a protractor or set-square to construct the following 4-sided figures.

(a)   Draw a parallelogram EFGH in which EF = 9 cm, FG = 5 cm and ∠HEF = 118°. Measure ∠EFG.

(b)   Draw a rhombus PQRS which has sides 6 cm and $\angle SPQ = 70°$.
Join PR and measure $\angle PRQ$.

(c)   Draw a trapezoid ABCD in which $\angle ABC = 60°$, $\angle BCD = 90°$, BC = 8 cm and CD = 5 cm. Measure the length of the side AD, correct to the nearest cm.

1. In the figure, not drawn to scale, CDEF is a parallelogram. CD is perpendicular to DG. Find $\angle a$.

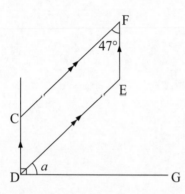

2. In the rhombus PQRS, not drawn to scale, QST is a straight line and $\angle SRQ = 54°$. Find $\angle b$.

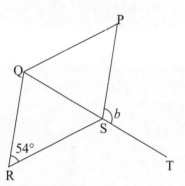

3. In the figure, not drawn to scale, MNOP is a parallelogram and OPQ is an equilateral triangle. Find $\angle NMP$.

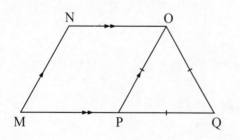

4. The quadrilateral, not drawn to scale, consists of 2 different isosceles triangles. Find the value of ∠WYX. Which angle is equal to ∠WYX?

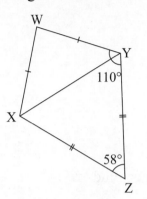

5. OBCD and ABCD are trapezoids, not drawn to scale. Find ∠c.

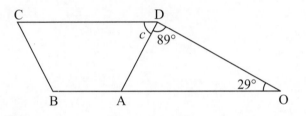

6. In the figure, not drawn to scale, ABDE is a trapezoid and ABC is a straight line. AE = AB. Find ∠d.

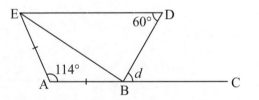

7. In the figure, not drawn to scale, PQ is parallel to RS. Fill in the missing angle in each statement below.

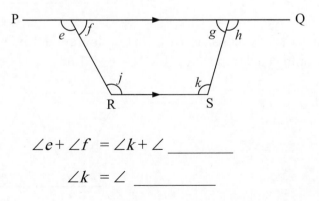

∠e + ∠f = ∠k + ∠ _____

∠k = ∠ _____

8. In the figure, not drawn to scale, HIJK is a parallelogram. GHI and JKL are straight lines. Find ∠GFH.

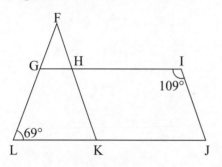

9. The figure LMNO, not drawn to scale, is a rhombus. Find ∠*f*.

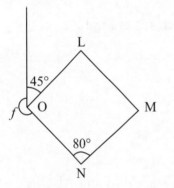

10. In the figure, not drawn to scale, ABE is an isosceles triangle, BCDE is a trapezoid and PQ is a straight line. Find ∠BAQ.

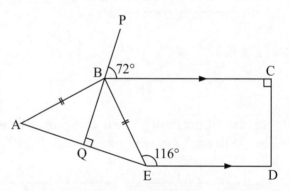

11. The figure, not drawn to scale, consists of a parallelogram KLNO and a rhombus KLMN overlapping each other. If ∠LMN = 63°, find
    (a) ∠*m*,
    (b) ∠*n*.

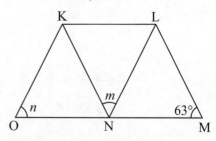

12. In the figure, not drawn to scale, PQRS is a parallelogram and OPQ is an isosceles triangle where PO = PQ. Find ∠SPO.

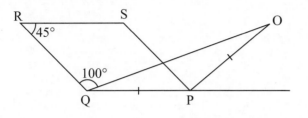

13. In the figure, not drawn to scale, DEFG is a rhombus. Find ∠DGH.

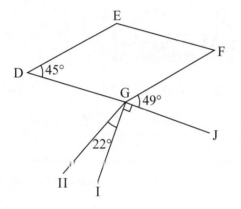

14. In the figure, not drawn to scale, ABCD is a parallelogram and CDEF is a trapezoid. Find
    (a)   ∠CDE,
    (b)   ∠FCE.

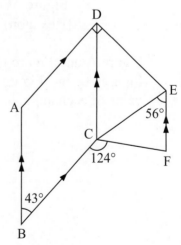

15. The figure, not drawn to scale, shows a rhombus. Find ∠p.

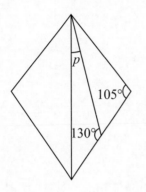

1.

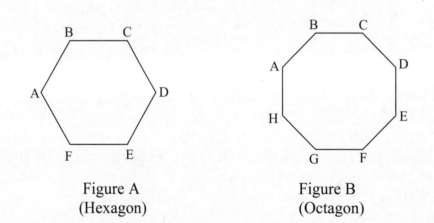

Figure A	Figure B
(Hexagon)	(Octagon)

Figure A and Figure B are 6-sided and 8-sided regular polygons respectively. Figure A and Figure B each has equal sides and equal angles. What is the value of each angle in Figure A and each angle in Figure B?

2. Three different quadrilaterals (4-sided figures) are shown below.

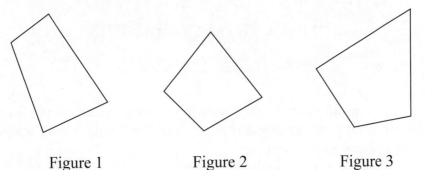

Figure 1   Figure 2   Figure 3

(a)   Join the midpoints of every side of each quadrilateral to form a
      parallelogram. Write the name of the type of parallelogram formed by
      the mid-points.

      Figure 1   _____

      Figure 2   _____

      Figure 3   _____

(b)   Can you explain why a parallelogram is always formed when you join
      the midpoints of the consecutive sides of a quadrilateral?

3. You are given 9 dots arranged in a square grid as shown
   on the right. 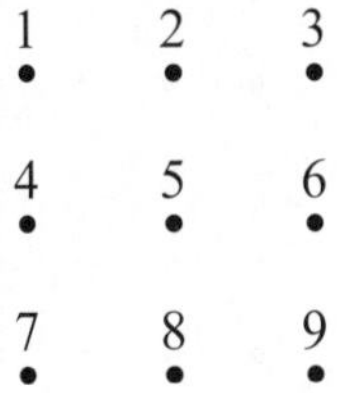
   Using these dots as vertices (corners) of a quadrilateral
   (4-sided figure), how many quadrilaterals that are not
   identical in size and shape can you form? (Figures
   which are identical in size and shape are called
   congruent figures.) Draw the quadrilaterals formed.

   Note:
   Using 1 corner dot only, we can form quadrilaterals
   1 2 6 4 and 1 2 8 4, but they are congruent.

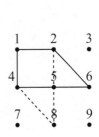

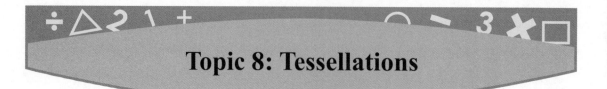
1. Draw and cut out each of the following shapes. Make 10 copies of each of them and arrange them together to form a tiling pattern with no overlapping or gaps in between the shapes.
   You will notice that a tessellation is formed.
   A tessellation is made up of **congruent** shapes (equal in size and shape).

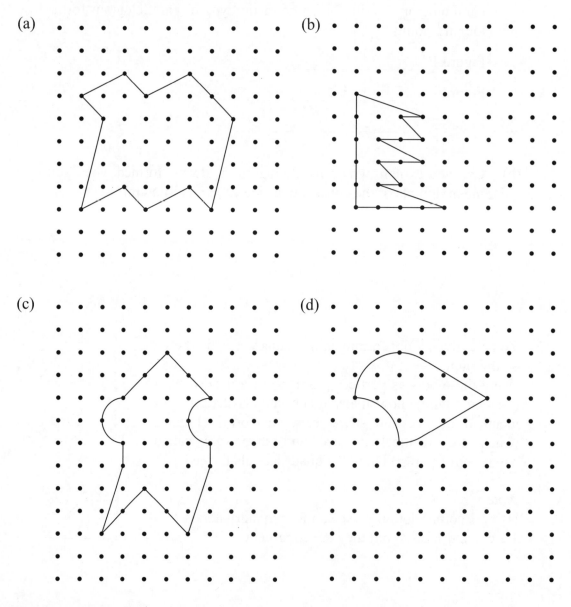

(a)

(b)

(c)

(d)

2. There are basically 3 methods used to tessellate or tile a shape.
- translate : Slide the shape to change its position but not its orientation (direction in which it faces).
- reflect : Flip the shape like turning over a page of a book (mirror reflection).
- rotate : Turn the shape to change its orientation but not its position.

Examples:

translate only   translate and reflect   translate and rotate

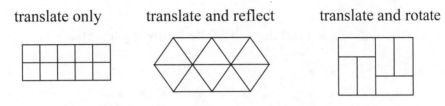

Determine the shapes that cannot tessellate in each of the following. Put a cross (✗) in the box below each of these shapes that cannot tessellate.

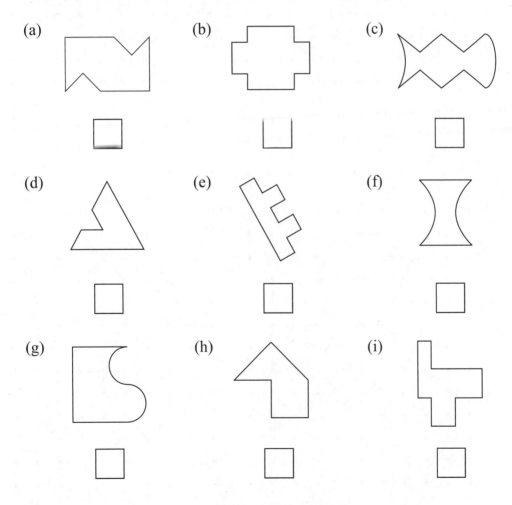

(a)   (b)   (c)

(d)   (e)   (f)

(g)   (h)   (i)

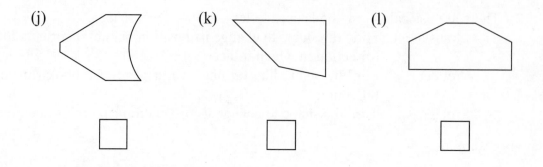

3. Shade the unit shape used in each of the following tessellations.

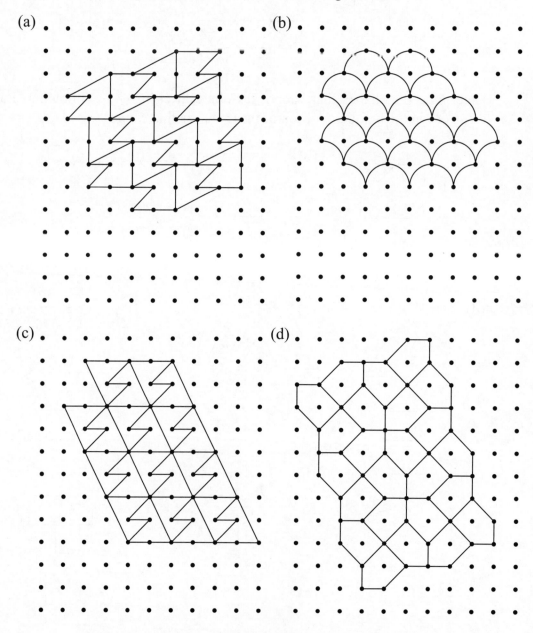

(a)

(b)

(c)

(d)

(e)

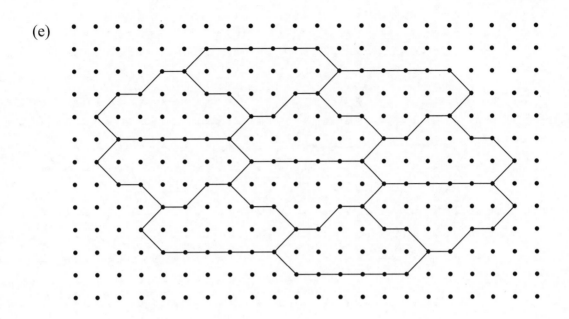

4. Shade the unit shape used in each of the following tessellations.

(a)

(b)

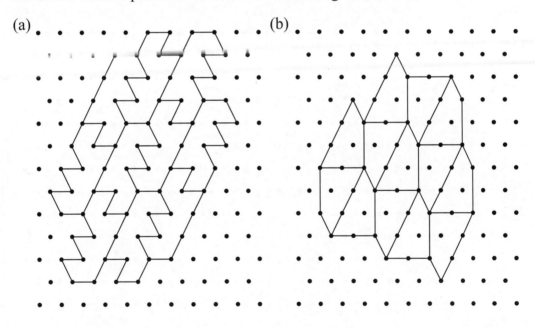

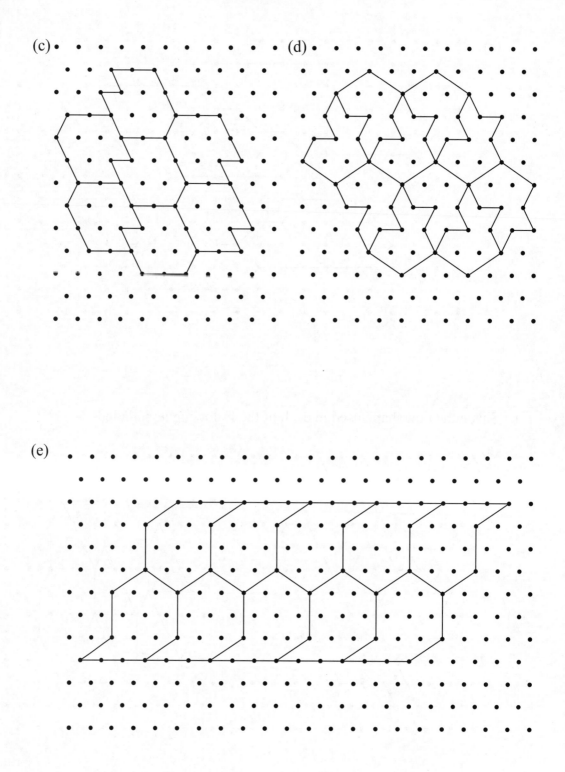

(c)

(d)

(e)

98

5. In each of the following, use the given shape to make **two** different tessellations by drawing 6 more of the shape.

(a)

(b)

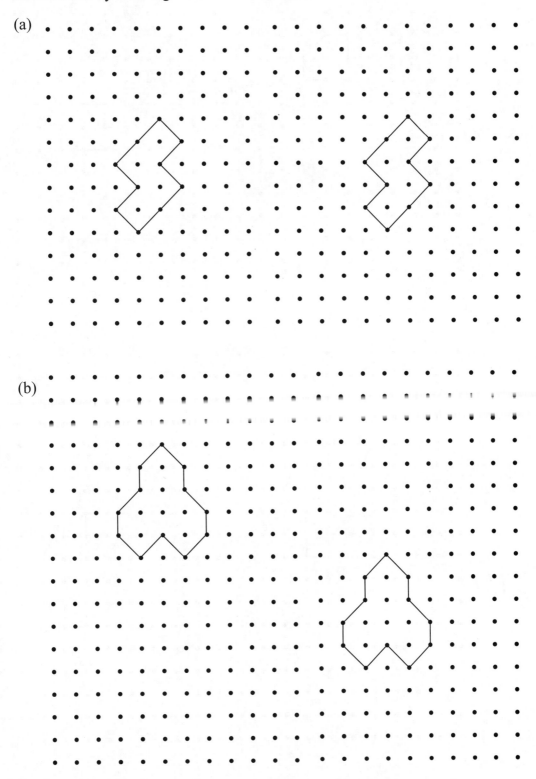

(c)

(d)

6. In each of the following, use the given shape to make **two** different tessellations by drawing 6 more of the shape.

(a)

(b)

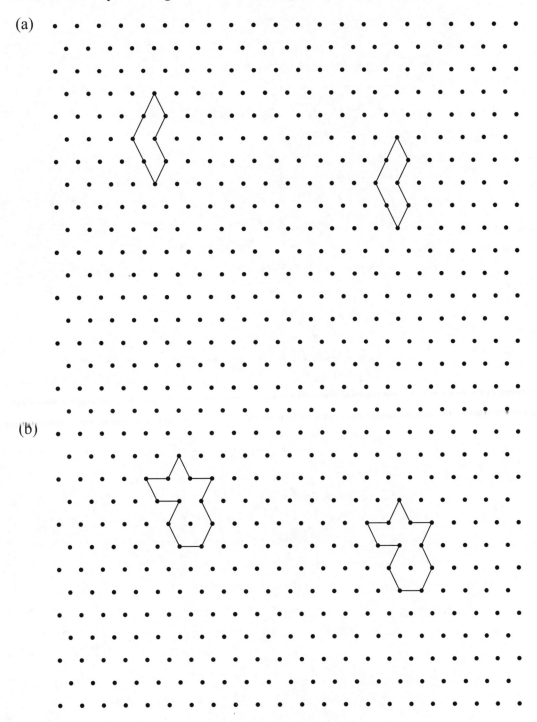

(c)

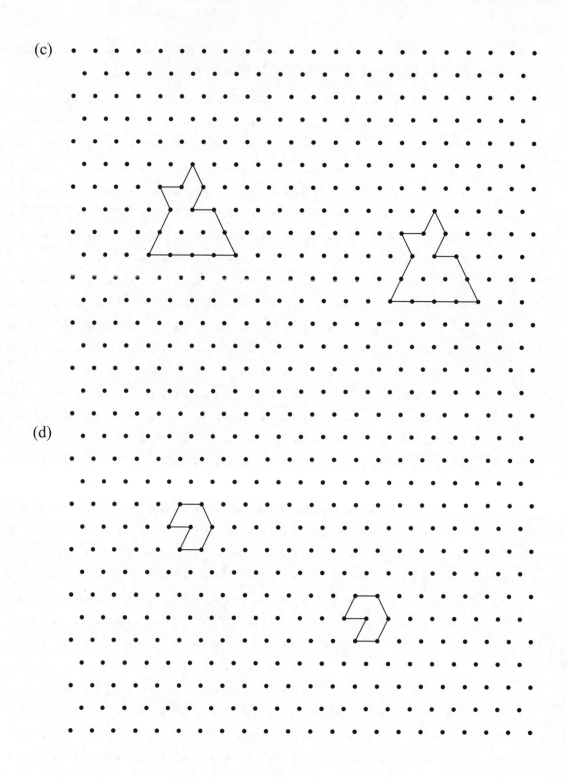

(d)

Take the **Challenge!**

1. In a tessellation, the polygons used will fit together with their angles arranged around a point with no gaps or overlapping in between. The only such regular polygons are the equivalent triangles, squares and regular hexagons (6-sided figures).

   A Chinese tessellation design called the Lattice Window of Suzhou is shown below.

   (a)   Complete the tessellation.
   (b)   Explain why the above mentioned polygons can tessellate.

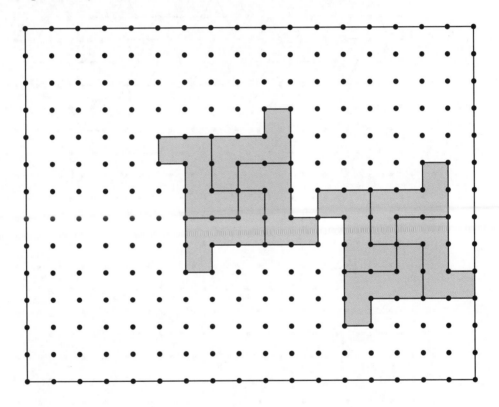

2. A Japanese tessellation design called the Kimono Fabric is shown below. It shows hexagon clusters.
   Can you change the tessellation to one showing windmills? Draw it below.

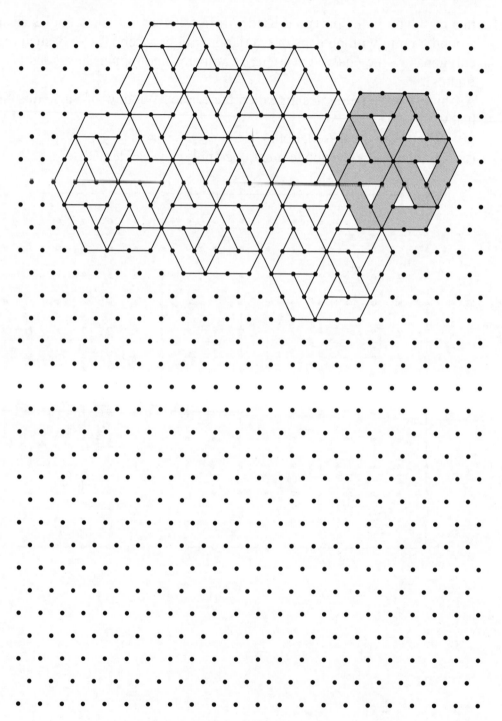

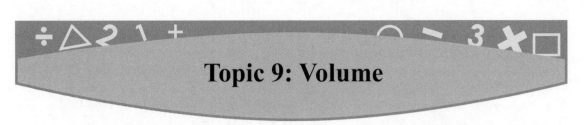
1. The following solids are made up of 1-cm cubes. How many 1-cm cubes are there in each solid? Hence find its volume.
(The volume of each solid is the number of 1-cm cubes it is made up of.)

(a)

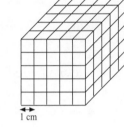

(b)

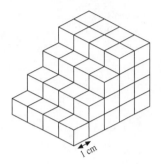

Number of 1-cm cubes = _____

Solid A — _____ cm^3

Number of 1-cm cubes = _____

Solid B — _____ cm^3

(c)

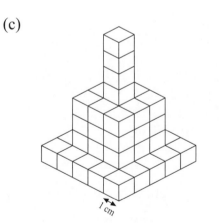

(d)

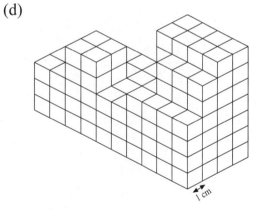

Number of 1-cm cubes = _____

Solid C — _____ cm^3

Number of 1-cm cubes = _____

Solid D — _____ cm^3

2. Look at each solid below. How many 1-cm cubes are needed to add on to build the solid to the specified cube?

Example:

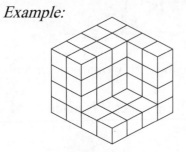

Solid E

Number of 1-cm cubes in a 4-cm cube
= (4 × 4 × 4) = 64
Solid E — (4 × 4) + (10 × 3) = 46 cubes
Number of 1-cm cubes needed to form a
4-cm cube = 64 – 46 = 18

(a)

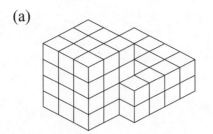

Solid F

Number of 1-cm cubes needed to form a

6-cm cube = _____

(b)

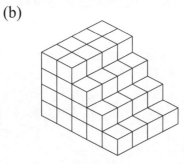

Solid G

Number of 1-cm cubes needed to form a

5-cm cube = _____

(c)

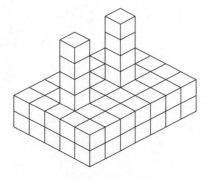

Solid H

Number of 1-cm cubes needed to form a

7-cm cube = _____

3. Complete the following table

	Length of side of cube	Area of each face of cube	Volume of cube
(a)	5 cm	$5 \times 5 =$	$5 \times 5 \times 5 =$
(b)	4 m		
(c)		64 cm²	
(d)			729 cm³
(e)	10 cm		
(f)		36 m²	
(g)			343 cm³

4. Complete the following table.

	Length of cuboid	Width of cuboid	Height of cuboid	Area of the base of cuboid	Volume of cuboid
(a)	8 cm	9 cm	9 cm	—	$8 \times 9 \times 9 =$
(b)	—	—	4 m	30 m²	$30 \times 4 =$
(c)	—	—	23 m	12 m²	
(d)	6 m	8 m		—	336 m³
(e)		12 cm		360 cm²	4320 cm³
(f)	—	—		1000 cm²	8 liters

5. Fill in the blanks.

(a)

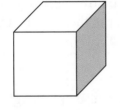

Shaded area = 49 cm²

Length of cube = _____ cm

(b)

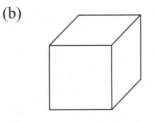

Volume = 216 cm³

Length of cube = _____ cm

107

(c)

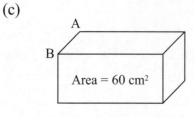

(d)

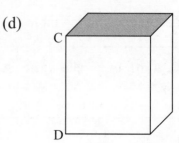

Volume of cuboid = 240 cm³

Length of side AB = _____ cm

Shaded area = 45 cm²

Volume of cuboid = 495 cm³

Height CD = _____ cm

6. Each of the rectangular containers contains a certain amount of liquid.

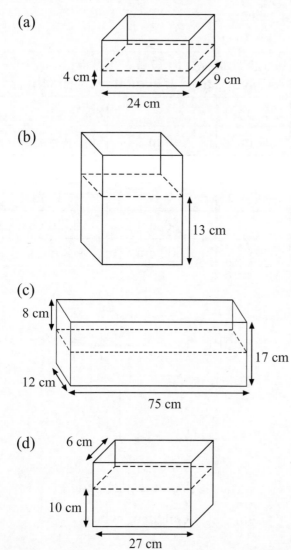

(a)

4 cm

9 cm

24 cm

Find the volume of water in the container.

(b)

13 cm

The base area of the tank is 77 cm². What is the volume of water in it?

(c)

8 cm

12 cm

17 cm

75 cm

The fish tank is filled with water until the water level reaches 8 cm below its brim. How much water is there in the tank?

(d)

6 cm

10 cm

27 cm

The tank has a height of 15 cm. If it is filled with water to a level of 10 cm, how much more water will be needed to fill the tank completely?

7. In each of the following, find the volume of the required solid(s) in cm^3.
    (1 ml = 1 cm^3)

    (a)

    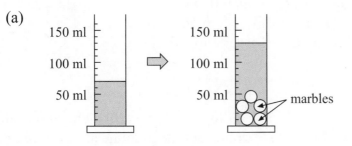

    Find the volume of each marble.

    (b)

    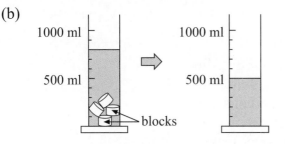

    After the 4 blocks are removed, the water level drops. Find the volume
    of 3 such blocks.

    (c)

    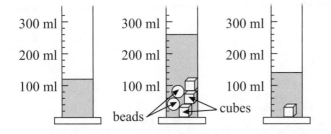

    Find the volume of each bead.

8. Each of the following problems involves a certain liquid added to or removed
    from a container.

    (a)

    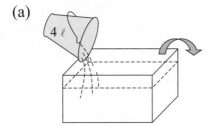

    The tank can hold 6 liters of water when full. A 4-liter bucket filled with water is used to fill the tank to its brim. However, 350 ml of water overflows from the tank. What is the volume of water in the tank at first?

(b)   A bath tub is to be filled completely with water from a shower head. The bath tub can hold 500 liters of water. Water flows from the shower head at a constant rate of 50 liters per minute. How long will it take to fill the bath tub?

(c)      The barrel contains 342 gallons of gasoline. A tap drains out the gasoline at a constant rate of 1.5 gallons per second. How many minutes will it take to empty the barrel?

(d)   The tank, when completely filled, can hold 372 liters of water. Water from Tap A flows into the tank at a constant rate of 16 ℓ per minute. There is a hole at the bottom of the tank and water leaks out at a constant rate of $\frac{1}{2}$ ℓ per minute.

Tap A

How long does it take for the water to reach the brim of the tank?

WORD PROBLEMS

1. (a)   What is the maximum number of 6-cm cubes that can be packed into a box with a capacity of 3600 cm^3?

(b)   A box measures 60 cm by 45 cm by 30 cm. What is the maximum number of 5-cm cubes it can hold?

(c) A wooden block 72 cm long, 42 cm wide and 36 cm high, is to be cut into cubical blocks of side 7 cm. What is the maximum number of cubical blocks obtained?

2. A rectangular tank 12 m long, 7 m wide and 9 m high, is $\frac{3}{4}$ filled with water. How much water is there in the tank?

3. A tank which measures 100 cm by 50 cm by 60 cm contains water up to a depth of 55 cm. When John pours a whole bucket of water into the tank, some water overflows. If the bucket can hold 28 liters, how much water will it overflow?

4. A container with a 15-cm square base and a height of 12 cm is filled with sand to a depth of 8 cm. 756 cm^3 of sand is then added to it. What is the total volume of sand in the container? Is the container full yet?

5. A container has a rectangular base 11 cm by 7 cm. Water is filled to a level of 12 cm. David filled it to the brim with another 231 ml of water. What is the height of the container?

6. A rectangular container 14 cm by 10 cm by 12 cm was completely filled with water. Aliyah took some water from the container to cook rice. The water level of the tank then dropped to 9 cm. How much water did she take from the container?

7. A water tank is 44 cm long, 25 cm wide and 25 cm high. Randy uses a 275-ml cup to fill the empty tank with water. If the tank is to be filled to its brim, how many cups of water does he need?

8. A fish tank measuring 1 m by 40 cm by 50 cm is filled with water to a level of 23 cm. A piece of rock is lowered into the tank and the water level rises. If 28 ℓ of water is still required to fill the fish tank to its brim, what is the volume of the piece of rock?

9. A cereal box has the following dimensions:

       Length   = 20 cm

       Width   = 30 cm

       Height   = 40 cm

To change the shape of the box, the height of the box is increased by 25% and its width is reduced in order to maintain the same volume of the box. What is the new height and width of the cereal box?

10. The rectangular tank contains 4.5 liters of water.

    When six identical metal cubes are put into the tank, the water level rises to 12 cm.

    (a)   Find the volume of the six metal cubes.

    (b)   How much more water needs to be added to the tank to fill it up completely?

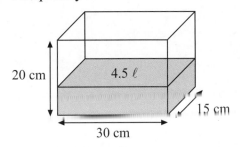

11. A metal tin measuring 20 cm by 30 cm by 40 cm was completely filled with kerosene. All the kerosene was poured into another rectangular container with a square base of 40 cm. However, 20% of the kerosene was lost during the transfer.

    (a)   What was the volume of kerosene in the second container?

         Give your answer in liters. ($1000 \text{ cm}^3 = 1$ liter)

    (b)   What was the level of kerosene in the second container?

12. A rectangular tank measuring 19 cm by 24 cm by 16 cm is $\frac{7}{8}$ filled with oil. When some heavy ball bearings are dropped into it, 138 ml of oil overflows. How many ball bearings are dropped into the tank, if each ball bearing has a volume of 6 cm³?

13. Two 10-cm metal cubes are placed into an empty tank, 60 cm long and 35 cm wide. The tank is then filled with water from a tap flowing at a constant rate of 10 liters per minute. It took 4 minutes to fill the tank completely. Find the height of the tank.

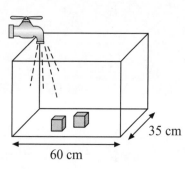

35 cm

60 cm

14. $\frac{1}{8}$ of a rectangular tank is filled with sand. The length and width of the tank is 25 cm and 15 cm respectively. Another 3750 cm³ of sand is poured into the tank, filling it to $\frac{3}{4}$ of its capacity.
    (a) How much sand was there in the tank initially?
    (b) Find the height of the sand in the tank now.

1. Which 3 of these solid figures can be pieced together to form a cube?

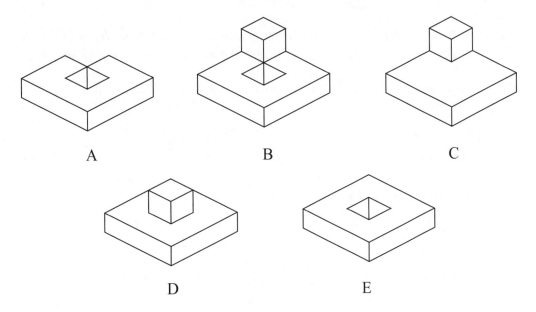

A   B   C

D   E

2. The diagram shows two identical beakers each filled with 350 ml of water. One beaker has 3 beads and 2 cubes placed in it while the other has 2 beads and 3 cubes. Find the volume of **each bead** and **each cube** in cm³.

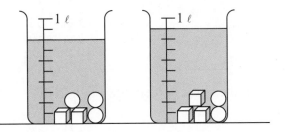

3. You are given a **square** cake. It is a two-layer cake. Each layer is 4 cm high and the cake is covered evenly with 0.6-cm layer of frosted cream at the top and on the sides as well. There is no frosted cream on the bottom of the cake. How do you cut the cake into 13 pieces so that each piece of cake together with the cream has exactly the same volume?
You can only make vertical straight cuts.

Section A

Four options are given for each question. Only one of them is correct.
Choose the correct answer and write its number in the parentheses.

1. Which one of the following numerals, when rounded off to 2 decimal places is 83.60?

   (1) 83.062   (2) 83.594
   (3) 83.602   (4) 83.621   (   )

2. How many sevenths are there in the fraction $3\frac{5}{7}$?

   (1) 5   (2) 7
   (3) 15   (4) 26   (   )

3. $\frac{3}{5}$ of a certain number is 30. What is $\frac{1}{2}$ of this number?

   (1) 10   (2) 18
   (3) 25   (4) 45   (   )

4. In the following figure, not drawn to scale, find $\angle z$.

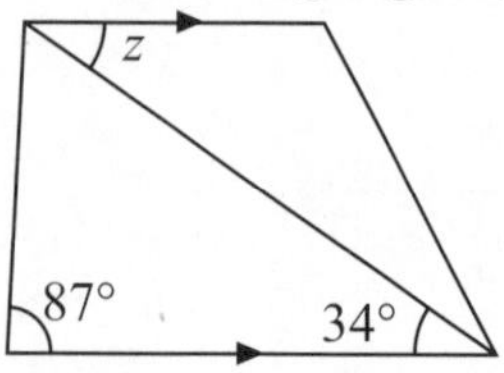

   (1) 34°
   (2) 53°
   (3) 59°
   (4) 121°   (   )

5. Express 12 minutes as a percentage of an hour.

   (1) $\frac{1}{5}\%$ (2) 5%

   (3) 12%   (4) 20%   (   )

6. A certain bank offers the following interest rates for savings accounts:

   > 0.375% per year for the first $3000
   > 0.500% per year for the next $47,000

   Karen deposited $28,000 in a savings account. How much interest will she earn after 1 year?

   (1) $105   (2) $136.25
   (3) $140   (4) $246.25   (   )

116

7. The following figure shows a triangle cut out from a 18-cm square cardboard. Find the area of the remaining cardboard.

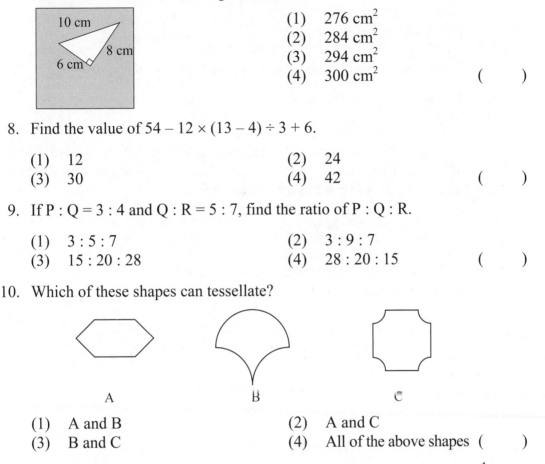

   (1) 276 cm^2
   (2) 284 cm^2
   (3) 294 cm^2
   (4) 300 cm^2 (   )

8. Find the value of $54 - 12 \times (13 - 4) \div 3 + 6$.

   (1) 12   (2) 24
   (3) 30   (4) 42   (   )

9. If P : Q = 3 : 4 and Q : R = 5 : 7, find the ratio of P : Q : R.

   (1) 3 : 5 : 7   (2) 3 : 9 : 7
   (3) 15 : 20 : 28   (4) 28 : 20 : 15   (   )

10. Which of these shapes can tessellate?

   (1) A and B   (2) A and C
   (3) B and C   (4) All of the above shapes (   )

11. Tim sold 0.6 of the oranges that he had on the first day. He sold $\frac{1}{5}$ of the remaining oranges the next day. What fraction of all the oranges did he sell on the two days?

   (1) $\frac{8}{25}$ (2) $\frac{17}{25}$

   (3) $\frac{3}{5}$ (4) $\frac{4}{5}$ (   )

12. Mr. Ford bought a new car. He used an average of 12.5 gallons of gasoline per week in the first 2 weeks. In the next 3 weeks he used an average of 2.5 gallons more per week. What is the average amount of gasoline Mr. Ford used for the whole period?

   (1) 3 gallons   (2) 14 gallons
   (3) 15 gallons   (4) 75 gallons   (   )

13. The postage charges for sending a package to another country is as follows :

| First 250 g | $3.00 |
| Every additional 250 g or less | $2.20 |

How much money must Matthew pay for sending his package weighing 2.5 kg?

(1) $22.80   (2) $30

(3) $55   (4) $66.25   (   )

14. A beaker contains some water. Its capacity is 800 cm^3. If a 350-cm^3 stone is fully submerged into the beaker of water, 100 cm^3 of water will overflow. What is the volume of water in the beaker at first?

(1) 250 cm^3 (2) 550 cm^3

(3) 450 cm^3 (4) 700 cm^3 (   )

15. Jack tied a box with a piece of string as shown. How much string did he use to tie the box?

(1) 102 cm
(2) 118 cm
(3) 236 cm
(4) 250 cm

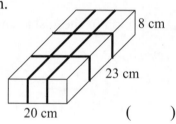

(   )

Section B

Write your answer in the space provided.
Answers must be in the units stated.

16. Express $3\dfrac{5}{8}$ as a decimal correct to 2 decimal places.

Ans: _____

17. Mrs. Chen had $\dfrac{8}{9}$ kg of brownies. She portioned them into 4 bags equally. How much did the brownies in each bag weigh?

Ans: _____kg

118

18. What percentage of the figure is shaded?

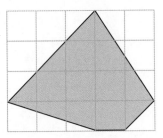

Ans: _____%

19. 3 badminton rackets and 2 birdies cost $78.60. If each birdie costs $1.50, find the average cost of a badminton racket.

Ans: $ _____

20. A sum of $2400 is shared among Alan, David and Shawn. If David gets $\frac{1}{2}$ of the sum of money and Alan gets $\frac{1}{2}$ of what Shawn gets, find the ratio of Alan's share to David's share to Shawn's share.

Ans: _____

21. In the figure, not drawn to scale, find $\angle p + \angle q + \angle r + \angle s$.

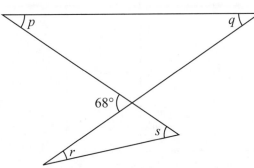

Ans:_____°

22. The volume of each cube is 125 cm³. What is the total length of six of them when placed side by side?

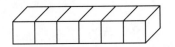

Ans: _____cm

23. On the average, Mustafa, Ricardo, Josh and Liam weigh 40.25 kg. On the average, Mustafa, Josh and Liam weigh 41.69 kg. How heavy is Ricardo?

Ans: _____kg

24. The figure is made up of 7 identical circles. What fraction of the figure is **unshaded**?

Ans: _____

The graph below shows the number of microwave ovens assembled by a factory in the last 5 weeks. Study the graph and answer Questions 25 and 26.

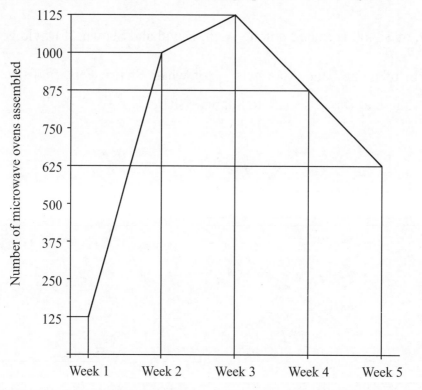

25. Which week has one-fifth the number of microwave ovens assembled in Week 5?

Ans: _____

26. What is the percentage increase in number of microwave ovens assembled in Week 3 from the week before?

Ans: _____%

120

27. A printing machine can print 1440 cards in 2 hours. How many cards can the machine print at the same rate in $\frac{1}{4}$ hour?

Ans: _____cards

28. In a class of 42 students, there were 4 more girls than boys. On a certain Monday, 1 girl and 3 boys were absent. What was the ratio of the number of boys to the number of girls present on that day?

Ans: _____

29. The length of a rectangle is $1\frac{3}{5}$ times its width. What is the area of the rectangle if its width is 5 cm?

Ans: _____cm^2

30. The number indicated by the arrow on the number line is _____.

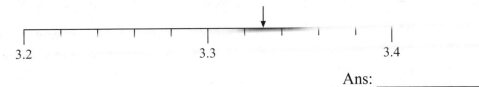

Ans: _____

31. How many lines of symmetry does this figure have?

Ans: _____

32. A rectangle is drawn, not to scale, within a parallelogram as shown. Find $\angle a$.

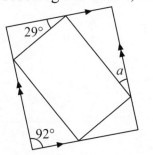

Ans: _____$^\circ$

121

33. Peter and Arnold share a sum of money in the ratio of 4 : 5. If Arnold gives Peter $120, they will have the same amount of money.
What is the total sum of money they share?

Ans: $ _____

34. $\frac{4}{9}$ of a class of 36 students wear glasses. If $\frac{1}{4}$ of those who wear glasses are girls, how many boys wear glasses?

Ans: _____ boys

35. The volume of a cubical container is 1000 cm³. What is the maximum number of blocks measuring 4 cm by 3 cm by 2 cm that can be placed in the cubical container?

Ans: _____ blocks

Section C

For each question, show your work clearly in the space provided.

36. Minnie travels $\frac{4}{5}$ of the journey from home to her office by train and walks the rest of the way. If $\frac{1}{3}$ of the whole journey is 6.35 km, how far does she walk?

Ans: _____

37. SPQR is a 4-sided figure. SP and PQ are two sides of the figure.

To complete the figure, draw two more lines, SR and QR such that SR is parallel to PQ and ∠PQR = 110°.

Measure the length of SR, correct to 1 decimal place.

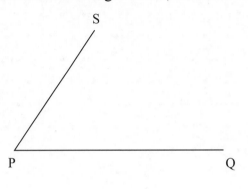

Ans: _____

38. $\frac{3}{7}$ of Jolene's monthly allowance is the same as $\frac{6}{11}$ of Wally's monthly allowance. If Wally's monthly allowance is $66, who has less pocket money and how much less?

Ans: _____

39. Use the given shape to extend the tessellation by drawing 6 more of this shape in the space provided.

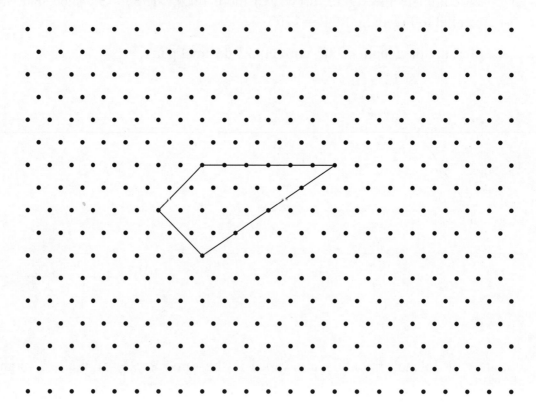

40. 3 notebooks and 2 pens cost $4.80.
A notebook and a pen cost $1.85.
(a) Find the cost of a pen.
(b) If a discount of 10% is given for a notebook, what is the discounted price of a notebook?

Ans: (a) _____

(b) _____

41. The graph below shows the stock of jeans in a store at the end of five business days.

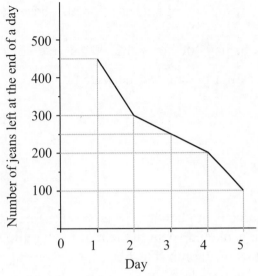

(a) How many pairs of jeans were left at the end of Day 2?
(b) How many more pairs of jeans were sold on Day 2 than Day 5?

Ans: (a) _____ pairs

(b) _____ pairs

42. In the figure, not drawn to scale, ABE is an isosceles triangle and BCDE is a parallelogram. XY is a straight line and is perpendicular to AE.

(a) Which angle is equal to ∠CDE?

(b) What is the size of ∠BAY?

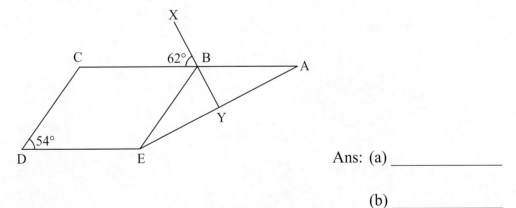

Ans: (a) _____

(b) _____

125

43. Hansel and Gretel contributed equally to pay for a $238 watch for their father. Hansel used $\frac{2}{5}$ of his savings to pay for his share of the present and Gretel used $\frac{1}{6}$ of hers to pay for her share. What fraction of Gretel's savings was Hansel's savings after paying for the watch?

Ans: _____

44. Winnie's allowance in January was $180. She deposited 50% of her allowance in the bank and spent the rest of it. Her allowance was increased by 10% in the following month, but her expenses went up by 15%. How much did she save in February?

Ans: _____

45. The figure is made up of three squares of sides 6 cm, 12 cm and 10 cm. What fraction of the figure is shaded?

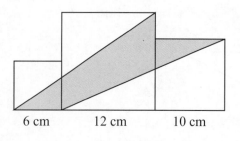

6 cm   12 cm   10 cm

Ans: _____

46. A tank 25 cm by 20 cm by 40 cm was $\frac{3}{5}$ filled with cooking oil. When 20 cups of cooking oil was poured into the tank, the oil level in the tank rose to 34 cm.

    (a)   How much cooking oil was added into the tank?

    (b)   How many more cups of cooking oil would be required to fill the tank to its brim?

Ans: (a) _____

(b) _____

47. A farmer reared some chickens and ducks. The number of ducks was half the number of chickens. He sold 136 chickens and 8 ducks were given away. As a result, the farmer had half as many chickens as ducks left.
How many fowls did he have initially?

Ans: _____

48. Alicia bought 205 pink and purple beads. She lost $\frac{3}{5}$ of the pink beads and was given another 15 purple beads. She then discovered that the number of purple beads she had was $\frac{1}{4}$ the number of pink beads. What was the ratio of the number of pink beads to that of purple beads Alicia had at first ?

Ans: _____

49. The rectangle is divided into 6 parts as shown in the figure below. The figure is not drawn to scale.
The area of each part is not the same.
Find the area of the whole rectangle.

24 cm²	20 cm²	B
54 cm²	A	63 cm²

Ans: _____

50. There are 97,500 people living in a housing development. $\frac{1}{3}$ of the males and $\frac{3}{7}$ of the females are children. The number of male adults and the number of female adults are equal. How many women are there?

Ans: _____

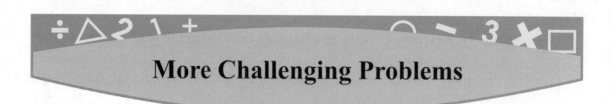

More Challenging Problems

1. A big cube is made up of 27 small cubes as shown. All the faces of the big cube are painted red.
    (a) How many small cube(s) are not painted red at all?
    (b) How many small cubes have one face painted red?
    (c) How many small cubes have three faces painted red?
    (d) How many small cubes have two faces painted red?

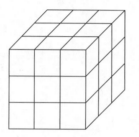

2. In a school, there are altogether 628 students from grade 3 to grade 6. Among these students, 316 are from grade 3 and 4, 358 are from grade 4 and 5, and 294 are from grade 3 and 5.
   How many grade 6 students are there?

3. Bryan's sister is trying to find out how many picture cards her brother has. Bryan gives her some clues:

    "If you add a '3' to the number of picture cards I have, subtract 4 from the sum, divide the answer by 5 and then multiply the answer by 6, you will get 12."
    How many picture cards does Bryan have?

4. Four piles of apples are arranged at a fruit stall. Half of the apples from the first pile are placed in the second pile. Twenty-five apples from the first pile are placed in the third pile. Then, half of the remaining apples from the first pile are placed in the fourth pile. Two apples from the first pile are then thrown away as they are rotten. There are now 68 apples left in the first pile. How many apples were there in the first pile at first?

5. In the following subtraction, fill in the boxes using the numbers 1, 2, 3, 4, 5, 6, 7, 8 and 9 to make the difference between two mixed numbers the largest. The number in each box must all be different.

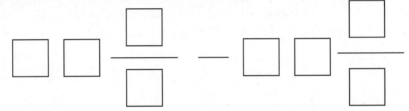

6. The rectangle ABCD is divided into four triangles P, Q, R and S. The length of the rectangle is 18 cm and the width is 12 cm.

   Area of triangle P = Area of triangle Q
   = Area of triangle R + Area of triangle S.

Find the area of triangle S.

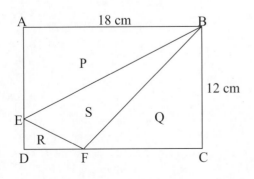

7. In the figure, ABCD is a rectangle.
   The area of triangle AEF is greater than area of triangle FBC by 12 cm². Find the length of AE.

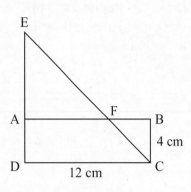

8. The area of the big rectangle is 128 cm². It is divided into four small rectangles P, Q, R and S as shown. The area of rectangle R is 12 cm² and that of rectangle S is 20 cm². What is the area of rectangle Q?

P	Q ?
R 12 cm²	S 20 cm²

9. The big rectangle is divided into four small rectangles A, B, C and D as shown. The areas of rectangles A, B and D are given. What is the area of rectangle C?

A 36 cm²	B 20 cm²
C ?	D 30 cm²